As featured on BBC Radio 4 Woman's Hour

The Art of Possible makes the impossible possible and
gives you a little bit of inner peace to boot.

STELLAR MAGAZINE

This book will give you the confidence to pursue the
dreams that you thought were impossible.

MIKE BUSHELL

Simple compelling narrative

THE IRISH TIMES

Editor's Choice,

FLIGHT TIME MAGAZINE

This is such a transformational read! Once I got
started I wondered why it had taken so long for such a
book to emerge – definitely a must read

JANINE WOOD

Buy two copies as you will want to lend it your loved ones and you won't get it back!

RENÉ CARAYOL MBE

Kate has a rare ability to recognise potential and possibility and she'll show you how to discover it for yourself.

SIR JOHN WHITMORE, BEST SELLING AUTHOR OF COACHING FOR PERFORMANCE

A mind-opening book

DIALOGUE REVIEW

This book encourages you to stop and think. Threaded with personal experience, what Tojeiro does quite neatly is to recognize that what works on a personal level also works on a global business level and that sometimes it doesn't hurt to think about you.

BOOKBAG

What's a book about new habits and the power of deliberate action have to do with motoring? Quite a lot it turns out.

EVENING STANDARD

THE ART OF
POSSIBLE

First published in Great Britain by Black Mustang Press 2015
www.blackmustangpress.com

A CIP catalogue record of this book is available from the British Library
ISBN: 978-0-9932369-3-8
eBook ISBN: 978-0-9932369-1-4

Printed and Bound in Great Britain by Caligraving Ltd, Brunel Way, Thetford, Norfolk, IP24 1HP
Typeset by Sheer Design and Typesetting

The Art of Possible is written and published as an information resource and guide intended
to educate the reader. None of the information constitutes a professional intervention.

Every effort has been made to obtain the necessary permissions with reference to copyright
material. We apologize for any omissions in this respect and will be pleased to make the
appropriate acknowledgements in any future edition.

The authors cannot be held responsible for any loss or damage suffered as a result of
complete reliance on any of this book's contents or any errors or omissions herein.

THE ART OF
POSSIBLE

KATE TOJEIRO

WITH CONTRIBUTIONS FROM
ARACELI CAMARGO MSC,
COGNITIVE NEUROSCIENTIST,
KING'S COLLEGE LONDON

For Tabi and Sophia

CONTENTS

Foreword   1

Introduction   2

PART 1
EXPANSION

Chapter 1.   Grow your brain   16

Chapter 2.   What is success for you?   28

Chapter 3.   What do you want?   39

Chapter 4.   Procrastination is okay   60

Chapter 5.   New experiences + new thinking = new results   68

PART 2
NEW HABITS FOR BRAIN PLASTICITY TO LIVE THE ART OF POSSIBLE

Chapter 6.   Random thoughts can provide concrete answers   82

Chapter 7.   Acknowledge your strengths in order to grow them   99

Chapter 8.   Capitalise on curiosity and learning   110

Chapter 9.   Use your talents to get unstuck   123

Chapter 10.   Attention to detail pays off   136

PART 3
USING DIFFICULTY

Chapter 11.   Shake off doubts   146

Chapter 12.   When the going gets hard, resilience gets going   158

Chapter 13.   Use your fear   173

Chapter 14.   Confidence can be built   183

PART 4:
THE NEW WORLD – LIVING YOUR ART OF POSSIBLE

Chapter 15.   Be happy   194

Chapter 16.   Be truly alive   203

Chapter 17.   Keep the momentum   213

Chapter 18.   Share & mentor   220

Greater Heights   225

Acknowledgements   229

About the author   231

Contact us   232

FOREWORD

There are books which inspire you.

And there are books which tell you how to.

The Art of Possible does both.

Kate combines lots of practical hints with real life examples from people who have achieved great things. She provokes thought but, better still, she provokes action.

This is not a sitting back in the armchair book. It is a leaning forward over the notepad book; a buckle-up book.

If you are content to be a "coulda', woulda', shoulda'" person then leave this book on the shelf. On the other hand, if you want to be the very best that you can be, you will find something in here to help you.

Rick Parry

Former Chief Executive of Liverpool Football Club
and former Head of the FA Premier League

INTRODUCTION

Everyone irrespective of talent, wealth or privilege, has to face down their fears, conquering things that we previously considered unimaginable. It isn't a comfortable process, but it is the 'sweet spot' we arrive at when we reach our goals that makes life truly memorable and really worth living.

What will truly help us to realise our full potential will be our ability to become 'comfortable with discomfort', a state of mind that allows us to overcome obstacles and explore new possibilities for ourselves. Be it a new career, a promotion, travel, adventure, learning a new skill - the list of possibilities lying in wait for us in endless!

Both personally and in business I am always asking myself and my clients: "Why do we make the choices we do?" And most importantly, "What drives us when we take a step up to do something we thought was impossible?"

What is it that motivates successful people? When they take a leap across the fine line between success and failure, what is the number one thing that they do differently from the rest of us? What is the thing that they think and then act on which makes them succeed?

The answer is that they get 'comfortable with discomfort', push past their boundaries and constantly expose themselves to new and different experiences, many of which can feel hard and gritty. This

'CAN DO' attitude ultimately enables them to really work their muscle of potential and to realise what is truly possible for them.

The Art of Possible will help you follow your passions and dreams and make them a reality. Through using the power of your brain, as well as your skill and experience, to greater effect, you can realise your own potential, setting and following the path to the life that you want to live.

WHERE IT ALL STARTED

"What on earth am I doing here? What have I done?" I thought to myself, or may even have said out loud, given that there was just the wildlife for company. I was sitting astride an off-road motorbike, a machine which frankly terrified me, half way up a mountain in the Pyrenees.

The challenge I'd undertaken was to ride for four days over the Pyrenees across several hundred miles of steep, rocky, wet, muddy, rutted and treacherous tracks.

By anyone's standards, this was a serious trip, and one for experienced and competent off-road bikers. The trouble was I was an ambitious beginner. In fact I'd never really ridden a motorbike until nine months previously.

To compound my sense of being out of my depth, I'd discovered that my travel companions on the trip were all semi-professional bikers, some of whom had competed against off-road heroes, like the three-time world champion David Knight OBE.

When signing up for this extraordinary trip I had been blissfully unaware of the calibre of biker I was going to be riding with, or indeed the gruelling nature of the terrain – fortunate really, because had I known the full facts I might never have signed up for the trip, which would have meant missing out on the greatest life lesson I've ever learned.

What had partly contributed to my decision to undertake this challenge in the first place was falling for Ewan McGregor and Charley Boorman in their TV series *Long Way Round*, which followed their three month motor biking trip across 12 countries. It seemed like such a wonderful, romantic idea to set off on a bike into the wide unknown.

But my main motivation for going on this insanely demanding trip was the heart-wrenching memories of the very poorly children I'd seen in Great Ormond Street hospital when my daughter was poorly and had an operation there some years earlier. The experience had left me determined to raise as much money as I could to help both Great Ormond Street Hospital and another children's charity. Learning to ride a motorbike off-road and get the trip sponsored seemed the perfect answer.

So there I was on day one of the trip, so out of my depth that it was laughable, yet having an epiphany of sorts. I'm no stranger to being uncomfortable; I've worked with many intimidating, and some might say, downright scary CEOs and business leaders in my time. But the difference is that in a boardroom one doesn't face the threat of seriously injuring oneself by falling off the side of a mountain through performing an ill-conceived motorbike manoeuvre.

Alone on that mountain, I realised that the only way I was going to be able to move forward was by digging deep. I asked myself, "What is this trip really all about?" I was discovering that this was just as much a journey on the inside, my inner journey, as it was a journey on the outside.

I am quite scared of riding motorbikes, though I love everything about them; the engineering, the noise, the smell, the sheer adrenaline rush and of course the bikers themselves. But a jaunt to Silverstone could quell most of those particular passions without requiring me to get on a bike myself.

The only real piece of sanity in my justification for being there was that I was doing the trip to raise money to help improve the quality of children's lives. The trip had been recommended by a fellow biker who, it transpired, had rather overlooked my lack of biking expertise.

As it was, I was able to complete only one day of the four-day trip as the challenge really was way, way beyond my abilities. It was the realisation that my lack of experience could put me, and potentially others, in serious danger of injury that made me call it a day. It was a decision I'm proud of, for during that day I had pushed myself way beyond what I had believed was possible for me to achieve, but I'd also had the good sense to stop the moment I felt that the genuine risk to my personal safety outweighed the benefits of continuing. And I was right to have sensed danger, as I discovered later when chatting with the support truck driver, for I learnt that hospitalisations were a fairly regular occurrence during these annual trips, an alarming fact I had hitherto been blissfully unaware of.

The fact that I was able to persist throughout that one day, way beyond the limitations of what I thought I could do, was the result not only of my own determination but also of the most amazing support, kindness and patience from many fabulous people along the way. Not only was I helped by the other bikers on the trip, but also by a hugely supportive network of friends and family back home.

I learnt a lot about myself on that trip, both the good stuff and the less good stuff, and it was a provocative and painful experience. At first, my having to drop out after barely completing day one felt like an utter failing. But when I had overcome my initial disappointment and realised what I had actually managed to accomplish during that day, with all limbs intact, I recognised that I was genuinely proud of what I'd achieved.

The journey threw up a lot of questions for me; questions and answers which motivated me to write this book. For I'd discovered that when something in our lives is really tough and yet we still manage to find a way to persist on through, there are huge life lessons to be learnt. Lessons that will take us on to further successes and lessons too good not to share.

Something clicked for me during that moment on the mountain, on my own with my motorbike, in a wood in the Pyrenees, faced with the biggest physical challenge of my life. Clients and friends had often remarked to me that I seemed hell-bent on doing things that frightened me.

I tasked myself with finding out what my own particular inclination towards overcoming scary things was. Could it be the difficult childhood, or something else in my past or in my nature? What was my own definition of success? Success, after all, comes in so many guises. The fact is that however success presents itself to us, it is what makes us who we are.

During that gruelling motorbike challenge, I learnt lessons for life and for business; lessons about facing fears and people, and the need to challenge one's way of thinking. But most of all I learned what it was to achieve what I'd previously thought was utterly impossible. In the weeks leading up to the trip, and right up to the night before, I was uncertain that I would be able to ride any of the challenging journey ahead. I had even called the guy who organised the trip to suggest that maybe I could do a different route! Used to dealing with very experienced riders he gave me his usual reassurances, without, I believe, really taking on board my lack of experience. The fact that this situation forced me to fall back on my own resources, including a need to be able to rely on my own ability to judge a situation, led me to make a number of important realisations about life. The lessons I learned from the experience, combined with my work with others who are prepared to travel outside their comfort zone, are detailed in the following chapters and form the bedrock of what makes successful people tick, lessons that we can all benefit from.

This book will take you through a process which will ask you to face down your fears, dare you to explore your emotions and examine those patterns of thinking which have the power to impact, either positively or destructively, on your life and your potential.

As you read through the following chapters and complete the exercises, you will be motivated to think differently, ask hard and challenging questions of yourself, and above all, strengthen your resolve and courage to do things differently. The following chapters will serve to inspire you to take the bold, brave steps you need to take to go further and higher in your professional and personal life. You will be brought closer towards accomplishing what you may have thought was impossible.

Through my work as an Executive Coach, as well as in the rest of my life, I have known some incredible, inspirational and brilliant people, who do the most amazing things, despite often difficult backgrounds or circumstances. I soon realised that there is a lot to be learnt from them. I've interviewed hundreds of people for this book in order to find out what it is that these remarkable people have in common with each other, and to be able to share it with you. I have spoken with elite athletes and other sportsmen and women, business leaders, people who are able to change both their own world and our world, people who have known tragedy in their lives and who, having survived the worst the world could throw at them, were then able to find a way through to achieve success. These inspiring people have all demonstrated that if we set our minds to do something, it is possible to create the environment, (however simple), in which these goals of ours can flourish.

Another important discovery I made was that alongside the determination and focus we need to practice, (and the reasonably fit and healthy body required to keep us 'on form'), we also need to work on befriending our brain as our co-collaborator. Recent studies in neuroscience show us that 'applied determination' can become a habit, a new way of thinking and a way of being that will change your life and the lives of those around you.

Thinking about your thinking, becoming aware of what isn't going to help you, being cognizant of how you think and really upping your general awareness will pay dividends.

Araceli Camargo, MSc Kings College London, is an eminent Cognitive Neuroscientist and founder of The Cube; a smart community of scientists, engineers and innovators. Her acute insights and expert knowledge, alongside my own observations as an Executive Coach, have helped shed light on how successful people use their brains to their best advantage. We know that we all have an enormous resource of brain power; we just need to learn to use it properly.

Through emulating what successful people are doing and achieving, we can create new ways of thinking that will build new neural pathways and allow us to act more powerfully in the here and now, ready to pursue a new path or adventure. By working our brains efficiently, whether in dealing with the most extraordinarily complex scenarios or the simplest of decisions, we will be able to see the internal noise - which serves as a distraction for the brain - fall away so that we can truly focus on what we want.

Neuroscience tells us that we can use our brain to change our lives, but it's up to us to choose whether or not we are ready to listen to this advice. The fact that you have picked up this book suggests that you are.

When you overcome something scary, it can turn the feared into something brilliant, a changed life.

All the tips you need for living your new life are here.

LIVING YOUR ART OF POSSIBLE

Atop that mountain, the endless opportunities that the world lays out for all of us suddenly became more vivid, vibrant and accessible to me. It might feel very hard to go forward, but I realised that it was ultimately possible, I had set out to do something difficult and actually all was okay; okay enough to carry on, for as long as I was able. Other things that I'd often dreamed of doing and being suddenly came to mind, along with the question "Why not?"

It was in that clearing, on my own, astride that motorbike, feeling uncomfortable in my surroundings, that the idea of *The Art of Possible* came to me, mentally, emotionally and even physically. The notion of *The Art of Possible* was the catalyst that wove together all my experiences of meeting and working with business leaders, elite sportsmen and women and a whole host of inspiring people, some of whom I knew and some complete strangers. The route one could choose to take to achieve success and fulfilment had suddenly revealed itself to me and it was beautifully straightforward. Finding a way of sharing this information became my very clear goal. Less clear was how I was going to get out of my current predicament, being faced with a rocky and slippery 45-degree slope which I had to ascend on my motorbike. Working out a way to solve this predicament was to be step one in the most important journey of my life.

Whatever the particular nature of your own journey is – one that may not require protective gear, a bike or a mountain – *The Art of Possible* will help you to prepare for it. It will teach you to accept that the road ahead may get uncomfortable and sometimes even painful, but that you are ready to embrace change and start your journey towards success.

The Art of Possible is a snappy book with an eighteen-step process in four parts, including expansion exercises for your brain and recaps at every stage. You will find tips, questions, exercises and action plans backed up with hard evidence from neuroscience, as well as real life success stories and observations gained from witnessing success in action. Peppered throughout the book are words of wisdom from a selection of inspiring people who live *The Art of Possible* in their everyday life; advice designed to keep your momentum going.

This book's purpose, in fact my purpose as an Executive Coach, is to get you to create challenges, stir up possibilities, look at everything that you currently are, so that you can then put a vision in place of where you want to go and get started on your journey to get there.

You will be able to refine your own Art of Possible by using the latest findings in neuroscience to understand how your brain works, and what it needs to function on peak form. Armed with this new understanding you will also be able to recognise possibilities within your world that you might in the past have overlooked, dismissed or perhaps just observed wistfully from afar.

The questions and techniques in this book will help and encourage you to develop discipline and clarity about why you are on the journey you have chosen, enabling you to get the results you want, faster than ever before.

The key methods of honing your skills and training your brain to realise your potential are detailed in the chapters ahead. Many of these techniques are repeated often because in order to develop, you will have to practice often. Doing something repeatedly will enable you to get 'comfortable with discomfort', allowing you to take your brain to the all important 'calm yet alert' state which allows for change. You will find that this change-embracing mental state is constantly referred to throughout *The Art of Possible*, reminding you of the fact that you really can develop your muscle of potential to its maximum effect.

This book is written in the style of a workbook and encourages you to use it as your journal. The stages aren't uniform in length or style, a bit like life. Some are short and sweet, some require a bit more depth and input, and each chapter includes very practical expansion exercises to help you train your brain and develop your own Art of Possible. This guide is designed for you to write in, doodle in, make plans on, and refer back to whenever you need to remind yourself how to live and love *The Art of Possible*.

"Everything is impossible until someone makes it possible" – Anon

NOTE ABOUT EXPANSION

When we train our brain in the right way, we expand it, which in turn increases our thinking power. *The Art of Possible* is entirely about using our brains to expand and develop the possibilities and potential in our lives. Physical exercise will also be of enormous help to you, helping your brain to grow, creating new brain cells, and encouraging you to think in a more expansive way, a place where you can be 'comfortable with discomfort'.

My first dirt-bike was a little Gas Gas 200, two-stroke, kick-start, and when in the 'power-band', it was mighty. To say, as a beginner, that I'd over-biked myself would be an understatement! I was intrigued to see that the exhaust pipe had a distinctively unusual shape and asked a bike enthusiast for an explanation. The answer I got served as a useful metaphor as to how we can get our brains to work so much more powerfully for us than we ever thought possible.

The 'expansion chamber' in the exhaust system of a two-stroke is quite incredible. Basically with the same amount of fuel it almost doubles the power output via a cleverly designed chamber that does something awesome with pressure and waves to create more power. It was invented by an amazing man named Limbach and re-developed by Walter Kaaden. It changed the face of motor-racing entirely, after motorcycle racer, Ernst Degner, who fled Eastern Europe (mid-race!) and took the expansion chamber idea to Suzuki, who then applied it to their own bikes, leading them to take podium after podium, and the rest as they say, is history.

The Art of Possible will act like an expansion chamber, maximising the potential and possibilities in your life. In other words although you will be surrounded by the same world that lies before you now, the way you now approach, process and use this information will be very different, potentially doubling your power both internally and externally.

The expansion exercises in each chapter are designed to help you train your brain and allow you to realise your phenomenal capacity, giving you the potential to realise those dreams that you may have thought were unreachable.

PART I

EXPANSION

CHAPTER 1

GROW YOUR BRAIN

Do you have a feeling that there is something more to your life, a calling you have yet to answer, a possibility, new adventures, a challenge, new career, new relationships? Does this lurking, niggling feeling involve something that you feel really passionate about, even if you don't know explicitly what it is?

Exploring and unleashing an untapped, maybe latent, talent within you, perhaps one that has lain dormant until now, is a very powerful and exciting prospect, a challenge that may well be just a little bit frightening yet one which you know will change your life.

The fact is that if we choose to look deep enough we all have many, many possibilities open to us. I will let you into a secret; the super-successful are not a different breed from us. They are simply ordinary people, like you and me, who have dared to look at what it might be possible for them to achieve, and have then, crucially, acted on it. Just like you, they feel fear; fear of the unknown and fear of failure, but rather than running away from these fears they embrace them. Taking that initial leap into your world of possibilities is the first and the most important step you can take into making things, big things, happen for you.

Does this make your pulse quicken? If this is beginning to make you feel excited, then you're ready for action.

STEP ONE: GET YOUR BRAIN ON YOUR SIDE

Many people fall at the first hurdle, simply because they get overexcited or allow the doubts to start messing things up for them. It is because these pitfalls are so common that it is so important to set up a framework for our success, getting our brain and bodies to work with us rather than against us. Creating a protective structure or routine for yourself, as you work on your foundations for your future, requires a little thought and some discipline, but it will also give you the clues and then the keys to unlocking your potential.

In order to fulfil your potential you need to harness one of the most powerful computers in the universe. And the great news is that it is right there inside your head, yours for free! A remarkable servant to all your needs, provided you can learn how to use it to the max. Yet to understand how our brain can work for us we need to learn a little about the way in which it works. For, like many new products that we purchase today, it doesn't have an instruction manual.

One of the greatest discoveries in recent neuroscience is the process by which new neuronal cells are created, a phenomenon called neurogenesis. The intricate mechanisms of neurogenesis are still being discovered; so far the process has been studied in the hippocampus region of the brain. The significance of the discovery is that it sheds light on how the brain regenerates itself as well as our infinite capacity to learn.

As you will most likely be aware, the brain is also constantly making connections and firing synapses so that when we learn something for the first time a new neural pathway is formed. The repetition of doing something 'new' reinforces the neural pathways correlated to the task, thought, or activity, allowing for an eventual new mindset or skill to be acquired. In other words the brain enables us to change and be more adaptive to changes in our world.

There are two ways that we can encourage our brain's ability to work at opening the doors of possibility for us:

The first way of improving your brain power, and for you to get nearer to the things that you want to achieve, is through hard cardio activity. If that statement fills you with dismay then admit it and move on, realising that it's time to start thinking like a leader. In other words, first acknowledge your negative feelings about the challenges ahead, and then set out to conquer them, energetically.

Intense cardiovascular exercise, specifically running, encourages neurogenesis to take place in areas of the hippocampus. To date studies have concentrated on the hippocampus; however, the hypothesis is that neurogenesis occurs throughout the entire brain and central nervous system. The other advantage of a rigorous workout is the flood of neurochemicals such as dopamine.

The significance of neurogenesis in the hippocampus region is in regards to memory and learning. Memory plays a crucial role in how we learn, as without retention and recollection of new knowledge we cannot progress in executing new things. In other words, neurogenesis reinforces the new routines and skills you will need to hone and develop in order to live *The Art of Possible*. In a recent study in the US it was discovered that the hippocampus does actually get bigger and stronger through exercise.

The body and brain are connected, and in order to move forward we do need to be in a state of action.

'Neurons that fire together, stay together' — it's a bit of a 'lovey dovey' way of putting it but is nonetheless true, as is the old saying "if you don't use it, you lose it".

But just exercising isn't enough...

"Reaching your potential is about being in a constant state of discomfort. The only reason that we feel uncomfortable is because it is new — nothing more, nothing less" — Araceli Camargo, Cognitive Neuroscientist

If you can get really comfortable with the uncomfortable, you've set yourself the perfect foundation for living the life of *The Art of Possible*. Your first step towards breaking out of your comfort zone and into the exciting world of possibilities is to create the new habit of doing something new and different every day. Incidentally, your genuine discomfort actually lies within your comfort zone. We often start thinking about our 'comfort zone' precisely because we are thinking about something new, which causes us a certain amount of discomfort. Yet once we recognise our discomfort as a welcome signal which alerts us to the need to seek out new information, we can see it as a route into the exciting world of possibilities. If your day is not going to plan and you metaphorically fancy climbing back under the proverbial duvet, chances are the comfort zone will no longer feel as comfortable. Discomfort is likely to be niggling there as you may have started to suspect that you're missing something interesting or exciting. Better to crack on with a plan and take an action.

Acquiring a new habit need not be particularly ambitious; it could be as straightforward as reading or listening to something that you wouldn't ordinarily choose. For example, immerse yourself in a topic about which you know nothing, be it recent scientific discoveries or gardening. Or you could simply decide to listen to a different style of music for a change, turning from Reggae to Classical music or from R&B to World Beats. Or make the decision to open a conversation with a work colleague who you haven't spoken with before, or visit an art exhibition or museum that you've never previously considered, or just take a different route to work.

The driving force behind your decisions should be that you've consciously decided to move away from your old, well-worn and frankly uninspiring habits and into the new exciting world of the unexplored. The novelty and difference presented by new experiences will immediately get your brain firing on all cylinders. Our brains continually search for the information that we already have; an easy, effective and of course very efficient way of going about things, but when we give them something unfamiliar to explore, they will work hard trying to process this new information and make new connections. Brainwork of this kind involves creating and strengthening new neural pathways and creating new neurons, both of which fuel and power our ability to reach our potential.

From my work as an Executive Coach to leading figures in the world of business and having interviewed many inspirational and successful people, I know this to be true. You may well be asking why a high achiever needs an Executive Coach when they are already excelling at what they do?

The reason is because high achievers constantly move forward, particularly after they've experienced a setback. They never rest on their laurels and are always looking for new ways to open up new possibilities. As an Executive Coach, I pose my client challenging questions, the same kind of questions I will be asking you in each of the following chapters. These questions are designed to turn deliberation into deliberate action, stirring up possibilities and enabling you to reach higher levels of performance faster and more effectively than when going it alone. Each and every one of my clients has succeeded precisely because they have learned to embrace the new, allowing themselves to get comfortable with new ideas.

Not only are successful people brave enough to get so comfortable with discomfort that they can allow new possibilities into their life, but they are also very disciplined and determined in their approach to reaching their goals.

Those that allow themselves to reach their potential do so by constantly thinking, both consciously and subconsciously, I may not understand this new thing at the moment, but I am going to work on figuring out how it works until I have succeeded . This 'figuring it out process means asking new questions of the world around you, looking for new information to assist you in your quest, searching out new environments and finding new people to help and advise you along the way. This search for knowledge may at times feel uncomfortable, confusing or even frustrating, particularly when one is faced with contradictory or unsatisfactory information. Yet the harder you work at finding solutions, the more you are feeding your brain with new information for it to process, creating new neural pathways, information and knowledge which you will be able to draw on when you need to.

Begin your journey by asking the right questions of your brain, present your brain with here and now questions which it can easily process. From something as simple as 'what new food can I try this evening?' to 'how can I persuade my boss right now that this campaign is flawed?'

Constantly hone your ability to ask the right questions of your brain, ensuring that each question you ask is absolutely anchored in today, this hour, this minute. If you treat this new habit as an important new discipline to be developed, your brain will soon reward you with greater and potentially more useful insights and information than ever before. And make sure that you also keep on asking other people interesting and stimulating questions too, as this will also give your brain more 'new and different' to work with.

It is true that most successful people appear to be completely at ease in their world, effortlessly evolving, embracing the here and now, accepting new challenges and developing their potential. But go beneath the surface and you will find that their serenity is really an illusion, for just like swans they are actually working hard to fuel their success with drive, tenacity and perseverance.

GET UNCOMFORTABLY BORED! YES REALLY

Boredom has been given a bad press, but the reality is that it is a crucial tool in unlocking your potential. Far from numbing the brain and leading to a lack of productivity, boredom can inspire you to seek out people who you wouldn't ordinarily speak to. It can even lead you to try activities which, under other circumstances, you might shy away from.

Boredom is an 'uncomfortable' feeling, and as we've identified, getting comfortable with the uncomfortable is a vital step to unlocking possibilities. If we remain content and cosy in our old familiar routines, sticking to the comforting world that we already know so well, we will never open ourselves up to new people and new experiences. But once we allow ourselves to wonder what possibilities lie out there, we will begin to accept that there is something missing from our lives. Accepting the status quo means living in an unnatural, stagnating state where we reject the new; whereas the real world in which we live constantly encourages us to 'live' every moment.

Unfortunately if we don't control our responses, we can go to the opposite extreme, allowing ourselves to become over-stimulated by what's around us. This overdose of stimulating information, if not managed correctly, can have some seriously negative health implications such as higher stress levels, lack of focus and creativity.

But if we allow a little boredom to give our minds a rest from the constant stimulation of technology, we will be allowing ourselves room to think more creatively. Creative thinking is an excellent route to realising your own potential. When we work our imagination, we are encouraging our brains to take in new things, have new thoughts and make new connections, which means creating new neural pathways and new neurons. And of course new ideas and innovation.

So, to get more creative and find your potential you have full permission to get a bit bored!

PERSEVERANCE

Once you are armed with new ideas and thoughts, spiced up with a bit of revitalizing boredom, the next step on the journey is to strengthen your ability to persevere.

The fact is that successful people thrive on hard knocks, because having learnt to persevere, they love a good challenge. When the going gets tough, the successful get going. Giving up is seldom an option.

When life becomes hard, (whether it's because we are learning a challenging new skill, a relationship has jarred or something has just plainly not gone the way we either wanted or expected it to), it will most likely lead us to become anxious, stressed or fearful. It is at such times that we are most likely to falter, admit defeat and focus on licking our wounds rather than looking for solutions.

As human beings our main objective is to survive. We have been given two main 'astute' systems; the brain and central nervous system, to ensure that we strive for our survival. The central nervous system and our brains are constantly assessing whether each new situation that we find ourselves in is either ' safe' or 'not safe'. If the systems assess that we are not safe or comfortable, our brains release stress hormones including cortisol and adrenaline to help us cope effectively with the incoming perceived threat. In short spurts these chemicals serve a very important role, as they change our body to be able to run or fight if we need. The problem begins when we hold on to the perceived threat and begin to ruminate. This keeps our brain and nervous system on high alert, which in turn keeps us releasing both cortisol and adrenaline. It is at this point that we begin to cause damage to cognitive functions and to our wellbeing. The sustained release of cortisol leads to disease as well as interfering with cognitive flexibility and executive functions.

When assessing the possible threat of the 'new', the brain is most likely to say 'not safe'. It is at this point that it will suggest to us a safer, and most importantly 'known', alternative option. But if we override this 'go with what you know' impulse and choose instead to explore the unknown, we are immediately offering ourselves up to the possibilities of new experiences, sensations and even successes. A bit scary, yes, but an infinitely more rewarding scenario than that of returning to the same old world of what you already know.

The good news is that opting for the more challenging, unfamiliar choices won't always feel so uncomfortable. If you stick at trying something new, however difficult it is, you will usually find that by the third or fourth time you attempt it, you will feel more comfortable with it. The reason why we accommodate ourselves to new experiences in this way is because our brain builds plasticity each time we try something. Once we begin to become comfortable with the uncomfortable, we are ready to move on to a more complex problem, then the next and so on and so forth.

Developing the ability to deal with both emotional discomfort and physical discomfort, is a great life skill to master. It is an ability we humans carry innately, a skill, which with a little attention, we can build on and develop further.

Once we have learnt to build the muscle of potential by accepting discomfort, new challenges become 'just' a problem to be worked on, rather than a terrifying threat. It is this very 'open to new possibilities' mindset which I have discovered in each of the many people I have interviewed and coached. And the good news is that this 'can do' mentality is available to all of us. Far from being something that we need to be born with, it is a lifesaving tool, which is relatively easy to acquire.

LIVE THE ART OF POSSIBLE 'GROW YOUR BRAIN' RECAP

YOU HAVE LEARNT AND DEFINED:

- What is possible for you.
- What your true potential is.
- How to harness your brain by constantly seeking out the new.
- How to get comfortable with discomfort.
- How to get bored occasionally.
- How to persevere daily.
- How regular hard cardiovascular activity builds your brain power.

CHAPTER 2

WHAT IS SUCCESS FOR YOU?

Write your own success plan. What is possible in your life?

"Without leaps of imagination or dreaming, we lose the excitement of possibilities. Dreaming, after all is a form of planning" – Gloria Steinem

For some people success is defined by status or material goods, whereas for others it depends upon sporting achievements. Then there are those who associate success with money-can't-buy experiences, or feeling safe and secure, or leaving a legacy, or becoming an inspirational leader, or being excellent at what they do, or an expert in their field; clearly definitions of success are different for every one of us.

It is very important to identify your *own* definition of success, rather than try to live up to a standard of success set by your boss, family, friends or teacher. Those that live *The Art of Possible* recognize early on the power of their own drivers, i.e.

what motivates us. Could your drivers be status, power, family, friends, money, excellence, how you live your life, where you have travelled, who is in your network? There are a myriad of answers to that particular question.

This is a pen and paper chapter for you to start making plans, allowing your brain to innovate and begin to define what success means to you. Any change or adventure requires a planning phase - so have some fun, loosen up, find a nice place to sit, grab your favourite drink and perhaps go wild in the stationery store and buy some cool pens and sticky notes. I like writing with an ink pen, but whatever works for you is what's important. One of my clients, the successful MD of a travel business, likes to go to the Pennines with his dog, and choosing a spot that appeals to him, settles down with his flask and notebook, happily planning for hours. His experience is that being in a new place with new stimuli facilitates the transformative thoughts necessary to start the planning process.

Drawing and visualising can also help bring your plans to life, irrespective of whether you are artistically gifted or whether stick figures are more your thing. When we visualise our plans, it often brings more detail and focus to the ideas behind them, which may serve to make our goals more real and do-able, or serve to identify things that we've overlooked.

"There are no guarantees to being successful. However, if you focus, are consistent and constantly train, it's got to make the odds a whole lot better" – Stephen Fear, The Fear Group

ART OF POSSIBLE EXPANSION EXERCISE

What is your definition of success?

Can you write down what success means to you?

Or draw it?

What is so compelling to you that feel that you must do it?

Just for a moment, suspend reality, logic, rational thought and common sense. Focus instead on bringing to life thoughts about your own visions of life. Use all your senses **fully** and make the vision as bold, vivid, vibrant and real as you possibly can. Try to listen in to your heart's desire in order to discover what you are really seeking.

LIVING THE ART OF POSSIBLE

We are sensory beings and often if we represent an idea in different sensory formats, for example pictorially instead of in written form, or even by imagining how something will smell, feel or taste, we are able to conjure up ideas about our goals that we perhaps hadn't previously thought about.

A very shrewd, driven, and one might say hard-nosed technology entrepreneur who I worked with, on being asked to do this exercise suddenly exclaimed "I smell the carpet!". I looked at the floor in surprise. "Not in here!" he said; "in the new offices, when we have 100 employees". He now employs 5,000 people across

the world. His olfactory system, or sense of smell, was especially informative to him, a key to envisioning a scene he dearly wanted to turn in to reality. So become aware of the senses that work for you, particularly the ones that inspire creativity or innovation.

ART OF POSSIBLE EXPANSION EXERCISE

I know that some of the following questions will feel like very odd ones, but bear with the exercise; you may well be surprised by what they unlock!

What will your success look like?

What will your success sound like?

What will your success feel like?

What will your success smell like?

What will your success taste like?

Establishing visions and actions is sometimes a bit like using a funnel with a filter at one end. Start off with big, wide, bold, even slightly 'crackers' visions, then feed them through the metaphorical funnel of relevant questions and see what comes out, refined, at the bottom.

Be aware that your big and possibly somewhat crazy ideas will often point to your truest desires and goals, so it's important not to start off by dismissing them as ideas which are too grandiose to contemplate, or as just plain nonsense. Chances are these ideas have come from your subconscious, not thin air, so don't be too swift to disregard anything just yet.

Think about the people who you will be encountering on your journey to the vision you have created, those who will be coming along with you, and those who will be there to greet you when you've reached your destination.

What will you be doing?

Where will you be living?

And now, to help you refine your visions and desires, which in turn will help fine-tune your goals and your planning, allow me to cast you into your future. It is important that you recognise the reality of this vision; don't think of it as a fantasy-land but as a very real point in time.

Now think about what your life will be like in five years (or twelve months if you find that easier) from now.

Write your thoughts down.

Or draw them.

The art of a good plan is that it will help you realise not only what you are capable of, but also how to take steps towards this goal with both efficiency and control. So remember that your definition of success will be paramount in informing your plan.

It's also worth recalling that great performance achieved through realising potential rarely happens by accident; in other words just wishing for something is not enough, major achievements are invariably the result of tenacity, planning and disciplined effort.

And as Henry Thoreau said:

"Never look back unless you are planning to go that way".

LIVE THE ART OF POSSIBLE
'WHAT IS SUCCESS FOR YOU' RECAP

YOU HAVE LEARNT AND ARTICULATED:

- What your definition of success is.

- What your vision is.

- How exciting this vision of success is for you. (May I suggest that if it isn't exciting enough you may need to start again).

- How to use all your senses (smell, taste, touch, sound, sight) to capture your definition of success.

- How compelling your definition of success is for you.

CHAPTER 3

WHAT DO YOU WANT?

Setting a goal gives us a focus and a destination. It is OK for your goal to change along the way as you progress on your journey. In fact your goal may turn out to be located somewhere quite different from the place you originally envisaged it to be. No matter, for the simple fact is that if you start off by having a goal or two, your mind will become more focused, which in turn will enable you to put a plan of action into place. Such a plan will then allow you to make the changes which will ultimately lead to you living your own Art of Possible.

Having an ultimate objective means that we are now free to begin our journey towards that goal, encouraged to go deeper into our, perhaps previously untapped, potential and ability.

LIVING THE ART OF POSSIBLE

In the late 90s, I met a young man at an event in London that brought together great technology ideas and money. I asked him what he did and he replied that one day he would develop a technology to find lost car keys. As I

wasn't entirely sure what to make of that, I don't think I answered him particularly eruditely.

He then went on to say that he and his co-founder were going to make every single piece of information in the world accessible to everyone irrespective of wealth, culture or location. It was so compelling I remember it as clearly as if it were yesterday.

The young man was **Sergey Brin**, who with his co-founder **Larry Page**, were the inspired creators of **Google**. Yet at the time I met **Brin** he was still an unknown, still operating out of a garage, but with a huge vision. Just about everyone knows the rest of that wonderful story and the power of big ideas.

Ask yourself 'What are my goals?'. Your goals may be huge, they may be small, or they may be a series of component parts leading to a bigger goal. No matter what your goal might be, just remember that simply acknowledging it means that living your Art of Possible is yours for the taking. As the song goes 'life's what you make it'.

We have one life to make as we wish, a life which offers us the opportunity to make choices, take decisions and risks and go for whatever it is that we want to go for.

I know that in choosing to read this book you have recognised that a world of possibilities lies ahead of you – so lets go get them!

LIVING THE ART OF POSSIBLE

Robb Gravett, former British Touring Cars Champion, was desperate to ride a motorbike as a kid, and his father told him in no uncertain terms that he would never sanction Robb's riding a motorbike on the road or his getting a licence. Respecting his father's wishes Robb still to this day hasn't ridden a motorbike on the road or obtained a licence.

He did, however, become UK Motocross champion at the age of 15.

He found a way of doing exactly what he wanted to do within his father's wishes and made possible what at first seemed impossible, through focused action, determination and achieving his goal of riding a motorbike. And he did it very, very well and then went on to become a brilliant racing driver, once more reaching championship level.

Many things seem impossible until we work at making them possible. The planning and visioning stage I have been encouraging you to work on within this chapter is about acknowledging the bigger changes that you want to achieve, whilst the goal setting stage provides you with the means to getting there. These exercises will enable you to carve out your action steps of your journey. Of course your plans may change along the way, but that's nothing to worry about; the important thing is to take your first proactive steps along your path to the possible.

When starting off on our journey, we also need to consider who might be able to help us along the way. We have a choice daily, if not hourly, of influencing outcomes; not just the effect of our own decisions on our own lives, but also the effect of our choices on other's lives. At a most simple level, a smile begets a smile. Lifting your thinking to a place where you stop to consider your influence and impact on others, and theirs on yours, will be invaluable in helping you focus on where you may need to get help in order to achieve your goals.

Explore your possibilities; what are the things that you can you be truly awesome or amazing at doing, and what are the things that you can just plain enjoy?

My goal was to learn to ride a dirt-bike and then ride it over the Pyrenees for charity. I'm really quite rubbish at riding a bike but I still enjoy it immensely. However when I get on that bike I honestly feel very much out of my comfort zone to the extent that half of me wants to get straight back off again. But once I begin to get comfortable enough with this discomfort, other possibilities begin to become an option. Even scary options like jumping the bike! Never ever did I think I'd throttle up and go for it, and yet I did and it was thrilling, and remains so to this day. Allowing yourself to get uncomfortable makes so much in life possible. Refusing to be frightened off by unwelcome emotions like fear takes us right to the edge of our capabilities and potential, revealing possibilities which you may never, ever have considered.

Part of your goal-setting will require you to do new things, learn new tasks and get comfortable with these new leaps into the unknown. By giving the brain 'new' information or stimuli be it through learning to jump on a motorbike or developing a five-year strategy for your global team, you will discover that being comfortable with discomfort always pays dividends.

I'm going to take you on what might feel like a slightly meandering journey. This is because we're going to explore new and different stimuli in order to define your goal more clearly. I want to start you off on the journey to the new and the different and to encourage you to actively seek it out.

Destiny is an extraordinary thing that many have sung, drawn and written about throughout the ages. It may at times seem the stuff of mystery, superstition and pre-ordained fate, yet in reality it can be as structured as it is ethereal. Provided that is, you allow yourself to take charge.

The fact is that each person's destiny is theirs for the taking. And why not? Let your aspirations paint the picture of your destiny, writing the story of what can be possible.

ART OF POSSIBLE EXPANSION EXERCISE

Don't overthink the questions asked below; the first thing that comes to mind will always be the most informative. The ideas that come from the front of your mind, in other words those that you access most easily, often signal what is most important and significant to us.

Are you in control of your destiny or is someone else? (Are you thinking too much about what others will think; friends, family, bosses, teachers?)

Do you feel as though you're bobbing along with the tide but would rather be catching a wave?

Having considered the questions above, let's now really focus in on developing those very specific steps which will act as a springboard towards your goals and get your journey started.

Sometimes we might conceive an ambition that, whilst desirable, seems completely inconceivable in the context of the world we currently inhabit. It may appear impossible that you might one day run your own company, get a promotion, write a screenplay, get fit. Yet there's often gold in these 'pipe dreams'. Far from being just fantasies, these ideas are the result of innovative and creative thinking and will have popped into your head for a reason.

Chances are that the idea your brain comes up with is something that will make you feel a little uncomfortable. This discomfort is simply a reflex reaction to being presented with something new and unfamiliar. Yet as we have identified, 'new' is something that is good for us, something we should welcome.

When a brain experiences the unfamiliar it gets to work on identifying 'difference', developing its neuroplasticity and strengthening its neural pathways. Each time your brain is exercised in this way it is developing your muscle of possibility.

So take note of the times when you are thinking about something that appears to be way off your radar, or something that you consider impossible to achieve.

ART OF POSSIBLE EXPANSION EXERCISE

What do you want in life, professionally and personally?

Imagine deeply …Is it a new skill?

Is it to feel more satisfied or content?

Is it to travel?

To live in another place?

To challenge yourself more than you have ever been challenged before, mentally and/or physically?

To be safe and secure, whether this is in the form of physical, financial, emotional etc. safety?

What is missing from your life?

If you had what was missing what would it be like?

What do you want to change?

What do you want to achieve?

What source of discomfort would you like to become more comfortable with?

"Life expands or shrinks in proportion to one's courage"
— Anaïs Nin

If it were possible, what would you do?

If you truly believed that you had the potential to do anything (if anything were possible) what would you do? These thoughts will signpost your goals.

Draw a picture or write a list: ideas, thoughts, doodles or all three.

Who will you contact? Where will you go?

How will you speak about it?

What will you feel?

Write it down, draw it.
MAKE IT AS BOLD AND REAL AS YOU POSSIBLY CAN.

What is your drawing or writing telling you? You might have to mull it over or come back to it in a few days and see what you think then.

Is there anything in there that you may have instantly dismissed as impossible? Is it really impossible? Really? Think again.

Now ask yourself "what am I feeling?" Are you excited, compelled, overwhelmed, feeling out of your depth, thinking "That's for others, not for me!" Write down your feelings:

1.

2.

3.

4.

Beside each feeling you've listed, write down what you could do, despite feeling quite uncomfortable.

If you've written 'that's for other people' ask yourself what they would do.

Then ask yourself, "Can I do that?"

How would you do it? What would you do first?

Moving from these ideas and goals through to action is the next power stage, and no prizes for guessing that this may also be uncomfortable for you too!

We need to accept that *The Art of the Possible* process goes something like this: comfort zone to goal, to taking an action, to discomfort, to comfort zone, to goal, to taking an action and so on and so forth.

If this seems daunting, just bear in mind that in accepting this process you are finally feeding your brain what it thrives on. And what's good for your brain is good for you both in the short and the long term.

MOVING FROM GOALS TO ACTION

Our brains like to absorb information (including your goals and plans) in bite-sized chunks, one chomp at a time. Nuggets of new information are far easier to process than great hunks of knowledge. The new information might be in the form of a new activity, a new way of thinking or a new way of feeling about something. But whatever the stimulus, each time knowledge and data are processed by the brain, new neurons and new pathways are created.

When we gather new information or learn a new way of doing something in a small chunk and then do something with it, and then do it again, i.e. practice, we strengthen the pathways. The more we practice, the more the new behaviour or knowledge will become strengthened through habit, routine or thinking patterns.

More importantly your new skills will be much easier to access, which will be particularly helpful during stressful or time-pressed situations. This increased accessibility of your skills will mean that you are far less likely to return to your old 'comfortable habits', i.e. your comfort zone.

Always break the big goals into smaller, more manageable pieces. For example, if you wish to run your own company what might be the first step that you need to take today? Could it be the step of working out how you can start your new company alongside your current job? Or to learn a new skill?

Can you break your goal down into little chunks? Where do you want to be in six months, three months, one month, two weeks, one week etc.? Reducing your goal into manageable segments means that the task will reveal itself a little more easily.

Thinking about each of the following questions in the context of your goals and actions will allow you to live your own Art of Possible.

Who will be there?

What will be going on?

You could be questioning your ability. If that is the case, my question to you is "What skills do you have already which will enable you to achieve what you want?" You may need to bolster them, but think about the foundations and abilities you already have.

Consider what it will be like when you have achieved your goal, and what existing skills you imagine yourself using in this future you are envisaging for yourself, e.g. communication skills, organization, efficiency, delegation, presentation skills...

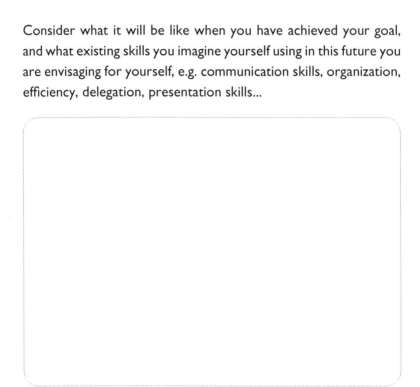

For each of the goals you have noted above, break each idea down into the smallest steps that you can, then working through your list, tick off each task as you achieve it, celebrate it and then move onto the next one.

LIVE THE ART OF POSSIBLE
'WHAT DO YOU WANT' RECAP

YOU HAVE DEFINED:

- Things that you have told yourself to be impossible which could actually be possible.

- What your goal is.

- What you want.

- Whether you, or someone else, is in control of your goal

- An uncomfortable idea that you would like to become more comfortable with.

- How to break your goals down into the smallest of steps.

- The action you will take today towards your goal.

CHAPTER 4

PROCRASTINATION IS OKAY

Now when we are thinking about the bold, the big and the exciting, it's not unusual for a bit of procrastination to set in.

"Imagination only comes when you privilege the subconscious, when you make delay and procrastination work for you"
– Hilary Mantel

That's thought-provoking, isn't it? And yet we often give ourselves a telling off for procrastinating or being lazy.

Procrastination can be our friend.

Your brain has all the resources you need to sharpen up your awareness, to notice your thoughts and to question them for greater insight into your possibilities. It is also very good at swiftly and efficiently finding the information and experience that you have gained in your life thus far.

Procrastination, like all brain systems, has many different functions.

One of its functions is to tell you that you need more information, more knowledge, insight or information. Procrastination could also be a sign that we are uncomfortable with the new, so we delay engagement. The key is to self-analyse and see why the procrastination is occurring.

Of course there is always the possibility that your procrastination is just laziness masquerading as procrastination. So one of your tasks ahead will be to know when and what you can do to harness your procrastination and give yourself the proverbial shove if you do discover that it's just laziness.

ART OF POSSIBLE EXPANSION EXERCISE

Let's consider that you may be thinking, 'But I don't know how to tell if my procrastination is just laziness'. My challenge back to you is that deep, deep, down you probably do know.

Cast your mind back to a time when you were thinking about planning and working on something and it was going well; a strategic annual plan for example, or a holiday, a change in career, a decision to re-train or even to start a new hobby.

When your plans were going well, what was happening?

What were you doing, saying, how were you behaving, where were you, who was there?

There was most likely quite a lot of activity; planning, making calls to new people, researching information, scoping out details. Can you identify exactly what it was?

Do you know why it was going well? Sometimes we know why something is going well and sometimes we don't. If we can't immediately identify why something is going well then we need to take a closer look at the situation and consider the elements of what was going on.

What was going well? E.g. were you hitting deadlines, finding the information, seeking out the right people? Write it all down.

It probably went well because you had all the information you needed and a good idea of what success would look like when it had been achieved.

Now think about a time when the planning and actioning was going less well and you appeared to be procrastinating?

Let's look at what might have gone wrong/be hindering you.

Was the task (the thing you were trying to get your thoughts around) too big for you to manage without breaking it down? If it was too big, e.g. running a new company, being fit enough to run a marathon or changing your career, your first step towards this goal may not be so obvious.

Do you need more information?

If you envisage the odd gap in your current skills (and you will, that's perfectly normal), note it down on a training needs list.

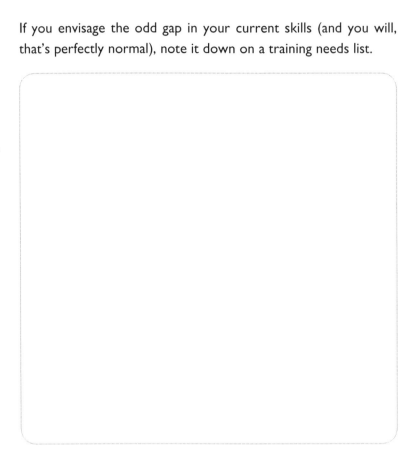

Remember that if you have been procrastinating it has been the brain's way of telling you that you didn't have enough information to move forwards and make a decision or good judgement. In other words the brain is saying 'I need more data' to make sense of something and act on it.

Through recognising procrastination for what it really is, you will be driven to gain more information and develop your muscle of potential.

LIVE THE ART OF POSSIBLE 'PROCRASTINATION IS OKAY' RECAP

YOU HAVE FOUND OUT:

- Whether you are procrastinating or just being lazy.

- Why you are procrastinating.

- What extra data, information, experience or learning you need.

- Where you can get it from. If you are being lazy, what it is that you are allowing to stop or hinder you.

- What action you need to take right now.

CHAPTER 5

NEW EXPERIENCES + NEW THINKING = NEW RESULTS

This chapter is all about finding new stimuli for growth, your growth.

What's your big idea?

"Better nouveau than never" – Groucho Marx

We brainstorm to seek a new idea or innovation. Yet conventional brainstorming (getting together to come up with something new) is ineffectual; it just doesn't work.

Big thoughts, big ideas and new ways of doing things are just that; they are big, they are bold notions born of new, different information and experience that enable the brain to create something new. They in turn will bring forth other ideas and visions of future opportunities and possibilities.

To have these great big, bold ideas we need to understand the brain's state of homeostasis, which is when our entire system returns to normal functioning range. The ideal state of homeostasis is to be calmly energetic, in other words when we are alert, energetic, and balanced. Achieving this state helps us stay open and ready to concentrate. When we are in this homeostatic state, we are not overly stressed, anxious or worried. We cannot avoid stress, but our ability to return to calm enables us to be more effective in problem-solving and sustains our well-being.

However, when you're thinking about the big stuff, including the new things that you want to do with your life, the ideas will flow better when you are at the point of homeostasis or concentration.

And as we've discussed, in order for our brain to work on building our future, we need to find new data for it to digest. These new sources of information will help our brains create new neural pathways and new neurons which will literally power our creative thinking. In this state our imaginations will be able to think big, the ideal context in which to plan our new desired outcomes.

But tempting as it is for us to become over-excited at all the possibilities that lie before us, we need to avoid over-stimulating the brain - remember those bite-sized chunks? For in order that the brain is able to process information efficiently and productively it has to be actively calm (homeostasis).

There are many advantages to being more 'aware', in other words focusing on being present within our surroundings, taking time to investigate what is going on in the here and now. A state of calm helps us sustain our attention to the present moment. Examining what is present, in the moment (as opposed to thinking about the past or future), encourages the brain to process information more efficiently in the most efficient context, i.e. right this minute.

We naturally get very tied up with the future (and often the past), preoccupying ourselves with all those 'what ifs'. However, once we recognise that the future is largely determined by what happens now, in the present, we can start using the here and now more effectively. Because the more we are open to noticing what's around us now, the more the world of possibilities and opportunities will reveal itself to us.

When I work with a client who is stressed, anxious or overworked, I will suggest that, just for a little while, they pause. I do mean pause, rather than stop. The fact is that the brain doesn't do stop unless something catastrophic has occurred. But if we focus on pausing, taking time to notice and observe our surroundings we are enabling our brains to receive the 'new' input it is craving, in manageable bite-sized portions. And it will reward us handsomely with creative empowerment.

ART OF POSSIBLE EXPANSION EXERCISE

Taking the time out to pause, even for just a few minutes, helps get the brain back to actively calm (homeostasis) and that means ready for anything.

Try it for yourself, use all your senses and note down what you can see, hear, taste, smell and touch.

Pause and observe the world around you wherever you are for two minutes, that's just 120 seconds. All it takes to power up the brain again so that it really starts working for you. The point I'm trying to drive home is that 120 seconds is hardly anytime at all. And the benefits are immense.

When performing tasks, from mapping an annual plan or something as mundane as stacking a dishwasher, the brain constantly looks for pathways that it already knows; patterns of habit, information that makes it easier, e.g. the spoons always go in the cutlery space. However in order to contemplate big, bold new plans and ideas the brain needs something new to work with.

So, when you are pausing, actually watch someone or something that you haven't noticed before (for example another member of staff doing their job, or just look up and notice the patterns in the clouds for a while) and see how your thinking changes; you will notice what a difference pausing makes.

By pausing your brain in this way you might find that you effortlessly have more new and original ideas than when you try to purposefully sit down and generate ideas.

Conventional brainstorming sessions occur because the participants believe, erroneously as it turns out, that gathering together and sharing ideas produces fresh new ideas. However unless new information can be injected into the meeting, all that will happen is the regurgitation of old ideas. The best that can be hoped for is that 'sharing ideas' will produce a new spin on an old idea, but it will still be a reworking rather than a genuinely new idea.

The fact is that without new data the brain can only use the knowledge of our experiences and insights that it already has. Sharing information is a bit like looking in an encyclopaedia together - of course there is a mammoth amount of information to examine, but it remains limited to what is already known, as opposed to something fresh and inspirational. In other words wracking one another's brains for new ideas is never likely to lead to light bulb discoveries, simply because there's no new data.

Similarly if we sit down, Winnie the Pooh style, and say to ourselves, Think, think, think! it is highly unlikely that under such pressurized conditions a transformative idea will pop into our heads. However, when our brains are in a state of homeostasis, engaging with an unfamiliar environment, the likelihood that we will begin transformative thinking is far higher.

So, to help inspire the big, bold and more importantly new ideas, take your brain to a state of homeostasis by first pausing to acknowledge your surroundings and then making a point of doing something different every day, a new experience to fuel your brain's power.

"The brain works in patterns and without feeding it new data or exposing it to new things it will continue to rely on patterns it has formed. In part it is for efficiency"
— Araceli Camargo

Expose yourself to new and different experiences and senses and see what they inspire in you. Change your usual and familiar radio station, take a different route on a regular journey, read a different newspaper, go on a different sort of day out or holiday.

So how can you get to your point of energetic calm (homeostasis)?

Think of situations when you are alert and interested, curious perhaps but remaining calm rather than stressed, over anxious or running late.

LIVING THE ART OF POSSIBLE

Some of us experience homeostasis after a run, or ten minutes with a cuppa. You might also find that surfing the net or having a little look at social media helps you.

One of my clients takes the lift to the ground floor of his company which is 20 storeys tall and walks back up to his office on the 20th floor, storey by storey, walking around each floor as he does so. A practice that is good for his head, good for his health and good for his rapport with his employees. During his tour he discovers and sees new things and new people. And when the weather is good,

he takes a short walk of about a mile and a half around London where his office is based, seeking out stimulating new sights.

What works for you?

The particularly cool bit about getting to your calm yet energetic place is that it will free up your subconscious, the place where (given the right stimuli) all your transformational and brilliant ideas are ready to be born. Find calm, find novelty and then unleash your brainwaves!

You may need to begin by experimenting a little with your state of mind in order to become more aware of when homeostasis happens for you, or you may be lucky enough to recognise its arrival immediately.

Once you've got to know your calm but alert state of mind, make a note of when you are most likely to experience it. When do you experience that actively calm moment; is it after your favourite exercise, talking with a friend, or when you are simply staring at a wall or looking up into the sky?

Write down those moments:

*

*

*

*

*

*

*

Write down what helps you calm yourself down when you are stressed. Since we often calm ourselves down instinctively, you may have to stop and take notice of what you are automatically doing to lower your stress levels.

When you're feeling overwhelmed or overloaded, particularly if this is something you often experience, you may need to build some time into your daily routine to pause and reach a point of homeostasis. A few minutes in the morning when you wake up, for example, or when you first arrive at your place of work.

Note down what you need to do.

For example, to achieve homeostasis, some clients make a habit of writing a to-do list for the next day the preceding evening. Your strategy doesn't have to be unusual or even dynamic, it just needs to be a rhythm that works for you and gives you that moment of pause and concentration.

*

*

*

*

*

*

*

*

*

Your mind may automatically be leading you in the direction of sweet tea, alcohol, chocolate or another stimulant to help you get to a calm place, but right now, to reach the big ideas you don't need the stimulants.

Notice when your brain tells you that you need to do something different, i.e. your thoughts seem stale or old, you begin to lose your focus or your thinking gets fuzzy. Now think about the best place to put a new daily routine in your day.

*

*

*

*

*

*

*

What's around you will make a huge difference.

In the big ideas stakes, a different environment is crucially important, because the brain works harder in a different space, one that is not familiar. Remember our Exec who goes out walking to find a new place in which he can stop and make plans. What kind of place would be different for you? Would it be an unusual, beautiful,

If you think back to the number of times you've come up with an idea or solution in the very last place you'd expect to have a brainwave (the shower, when walking your dog, whilst playing sport, travelling, or on holiday), you'll know this to be true. Your light-bulb moment happened because your environment had encouraged your brain to be actively calm (at homeostasis), ready for anything including responding more effectively to different things.

New stimuli will create the new bold and transformative thinking necessary for you to enter the next stage of your life.

Decide to train your brain to seek out the 'new' and enhance your ability to live *The Art of Possible*.

LIVE THE ART OF POSSIBLE
'NEW EXPERIENCE + NEW THINKING = NEW RESULTS' RECAP

YOU HAVE DISCOVERED HOW IMPORTANT IT IS TO:

- Seek out new experience, data, information, environment or learning in order to up the stakes on your creative and innovative thinking.

- Pause regularly to check in on the world (see the view, hear the voices, feel the breeze, smell the roses, taste the coffee).

- Change one of your routines to enhance your thinking.

- Identify how you calm down.

- Add a new daily routine to get you to that place of calm but energetic place (homeostasis).

PART 2

NEW HABITS FOR BRAIN PLASTICITY TO LIVE THE ART OF POSSIBLE

CHAPTER 6

RANDOM THOUGHTS CAN PROVIDE CONCRETE ANSWERS

This chapter is about paying attention to random thoughts, thoughts which may prove to be powerful indicators of what is possible for you.

"Reach high, for stars lie hidden in your soul. Dream deep, for every dream precedes the goal" – Pamela Vaull Starr

There is certainly much to learn about why and how we dream, many asserting that a dream is your subconscious mind communicating with you. Certainly dreams can be quite informative about our conscious thoughts, showing us the way towards the things that we are seeking.

There are two types of dream, the dream that happens when we are asleep and our daydreams. We shall focus on our daydreams which can often be incredibly informative and often easier to access.

Paying attention to your daydreams may seem fanciful, particularly if you believe them to be unreachable castles in the sky. But what if you began to take these daydreams seriously? What if you recognised them as manifestations of desires that you'd hidden or buried because they seemed impossible, either now or in the future?

Those dreams that we tend to inhibit with discouraging conditionals like the wistful 'if only...' or half-hearted 'perhaps', as in "if only I was fit enough, could save some money, could be more confident" or "perhaps if I retrained, got a new job, became a bit happier.....". These inhibitors that we so easily put in our way have a great ability to keep us stuck. Yes, our dreams are sometimes very different to our lives as we currently live them, and may even feel uncomfortable when we dare to consider them seriously, but that's exactly why it is important to notice and recognise them. Clocking these signals from your subconscious will help you practice thinking more expansively about what you want to change. It will also allow you to focus on the here and now, and be rid of the shackles of your past experience, or those inhibiting, naysaying rules that we set for ourselves. Those negative, warning voices inside our head that say, "But I could never run a business, no-one in my family could win a gold medal, someone like me would never be famous / go to university / have a great relationship" or just the "I'd probably fail so there's no point trying".

Wouldn't it be so much more productive to ask ourselves, Why the hell not?!

Some of the highly successful people whom I have interviewed have lofty daydreams, but rather than dismissing them they welcome these visions as a signpost or foundation for what they are looking to do next or search for.

The fact is that if we carry on dismissing our daydreams as just wistful whimsies we will remain firmly where we are. We may even justify our negativity with statements such as "Well that's something someone else would do, it's not for me". Not surprisingly the brain can't work with negativity. But if we fuel it with a question, allowing it to latch onto possibilities, it will be eager to collaborate with us to make these dreams come true.

How exciting to realise that far from being time-wasting distractions, daydreams are actually giving you a window on how you could achieve your big goals, desires and the experiences you've been yearning for.

This chapter shows you how to tap into some of that subconscious thinking which presents itself to you in your daydreams. It will give you techniques for developing the rigour and discipline to ask your brain helpful questions, rather than dismissive statements. And moreover it will help you understand the power of 'Now'!

Daydreams of course may be just a few minutes or moments in a busy day while we wait for someone or something, or just happen to not be occupied for a few moments.

"What we do today can improve all of our tomorrows"
– Anon

So, if these daydreams are giving you an insight or signpost to an unfulfilled desire or passion, what do you need to do now to make these wishes a possibility?

ART OF POSSIBLE EXPANSION EXERCISE

"Any dream worth dreaming, is worth the effort to make it come true." – Evan Gourley

Answer the following questions:

Next time you find yourself daydreaming and filling your mind with 'what ifs?', stop for a moment to think about it.

Is there a recurring thought or desire in your daydreams?

What do you find interesting about that?

Is there someone in your daydreams that you don't know?

What can you learn from the dream?

Do you know anything already of what you are daydreaming about?

What might your daydream be representing?

This might seem nonsensical to you; however thinking widely, broadly and creatively in this way means that you will be unleashing ideas, and the germ of 'what's next' for you is more likely to be revealed.

Visualise what's in your daydream more completely.

Think about those passions that are ignited when you daydream.

Does your daydream include a specific activity, either one you are doing on your own, or with a group of people or a certain person?

Where are you in your daydream; in your home or somewhere else familiar to you, or are you someplace unknown to you or abroad?

Remember the best way to ensure that our brains work with us is to get more comfortable with discomfort, i.e. seeking out new experiences, new environments and new data. And to focus on being in the moment. Today. Now.

So is there anything about your daydreams that makes you feel slightly uncomfortable but perhaps a little excited too? Write it all down.

Or draw it:

Some of your big ideas and goals will be found in these observations.

Now, once we've filtered out the inhibiting 'if onlys' or the 'maybe one day when I'm readys' and are left with our big statement such as 'I want to run a company, complete a marathon, get fit, find a partner' we are ready to begin focusing. This is where disciplined thinking comes in. We are now ready to turn the big statements into a series of small questions for the brain to start working on, right away, in the here and now. For it is this disciplined way of processing your dreams into bite-sized chunks that will help change your life. You are about to turn your airy dreams into a very real action plan.

Are you asking the right questions?

To make the things you desire more likely to become a possibility, consider what you want to ask your key collaborator, your brain?

To harness the power of our brains it is crucial that we develop the skill of asking the right questions. If we ask a question in the here and now, rather than one that involves referring to past or future events, the brain will look outside itself, searching and receiving information from the immediate environment it finds itself in.

The brain needs to work on questions not statements. Give it a statement and it will give you back another statement, a little different from yours perhaps but a statement nonetheless, rather than an answer. Don't discount statements entirely as they are often valuable and often surprisingly bold, but be careful not to create a never-ending spiral that means the brain works on searching and retrieving old information. The brain doesn't like ambiguity, it needs somewhere to go, as do we!

Now examine what you have written down, and begin to turn it into an action plan for the coming week.

What is the first step that you can take? All great journeys always, always start with just one small first step.

Look at the skills you already have, the condition you are in right now, and work out what you need to build on, step by step, towards your goal.

For example, if you want to run a marathon, how fit are you? How far can you run? What do you need to do to build up to running a marathon?

Or, if you want to run a company, what do you already know about the kind of company you want to run? How can you build on this knowledge? Where would you like it to be? What would you like it to do?

What do you need to do right now to get closer to achieving your dream?

It may be a phone call, a bit of research, asking someone to help with your day to day professional or personal responsibilities?

When will you do it?

The answer should ideally be now, but if you feel yourself procrastinating, remember that it is simply your brain requesting more information, which you are now in a position to look for and find. And if it isn't procrastination, just go do it!

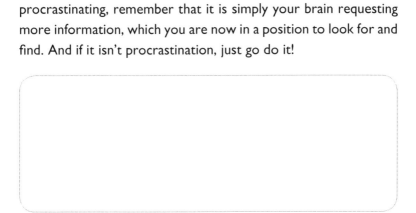

You will now be the proud owner of a very real action plan for turning what is possible into what you want to make happen. You will also have a far clearer idea of when and how you are going to get there and, very importantly, how you will start this journey.

Araceli Camargo likens the brain to a reliable golden retriever dog. Throw the dog a ball and it will bring it back. Every time. Ask the right question and the brain will bring you back the right answer. Every time.

But remember that in order for the brain to retrieve and find information for us that will spark a new and dynamic way of thinking, we need to ask the brain a question about 'now', preferably within new surroundings.

So, how do you ask the right question of your brain? Here's an example; say in five years you want to be running your own successful business, how do you present this as a 'useful' question to the brain?

Regardless of what kind of business you want, your brain will get stuck on the concept of five years because it can't compute time in this way, but if you give it a concrete question like I want to run my own business, what should I do now to start the ball rolling? it will identify with the here and now and deliver you an answer.

If fate deems that you almost get knocked over by a bus in five years time, your brain can do zip about it now. However, if the accident looks like it's about to happen right this second, the brain will coordinate the mind and body to ensure that you will do everything within your power to ensure your survival. Which is why we need to ask our brains, What do I need to do in the here and now to make my business successful? Regardless of whether or not we estimate that it will take five years to launch it.

So, using the ideas thrown up by your dreams, focus on asking the brain questions like:

What is it that I'd really like to do or achieve? What can I do to start making it happen? What can I do to start the journey?

Where can I get the skills, time, resources etc. to achieve what I want to do?

These questions will allow the brain to bring back useful, top quality answers, including suggestions as to how you can find out the new data that you need. Believe me, the help is all there in your No.1 collaborator, the phenomenal computer that is your brain!

Keep in mind the fact that the brain is set to react to 'now'; worrying about past mistakes or future challenges will only confuse and distract it.

So if you really want to think about what is possible for you, think about it now, right now and in the context of your world, today.

This kind of clear thinking, unmuddied by past or future worries, will lead you straight to your big goal and allow you to unlock your potential.

Reacting to the here and now is essentially what mindfulness is all about.

Mindfulness – the art of being present – has long been proven to make a difference to decision-making, stress levels and indeed happiness. There is much new data about mindfulness being a cure for (non-chronic) depression. Neuroscientists have now proven that mindfulness, or being in the 'now' works brilliantly at harnessing our own brain power too.

Mindfulness is a discipline that will allow you to build the muscle of 'being in the present'. When you are in the moment you will be more able to seek out and find new information, that difference that your brain finds so nourishing, building neuroplasticity and creating new neurons. In other words the ability to be mindful means that we are training the brain to be more comfortable with discomfort, practising *The Art of Possible*.

A note on your definition of success, what's possible for you and why this might feel a bit too daunting for you right now:

You are bold, brilliant and brave – of course you are, you wouldn't be reading this book if you weren't ready to take control of your own destiny with courage and creativity.

It's now time to hone in on *The Art of Possible* and start making your dreams a reality.

Start off by adding some more details to the questions you have already answered. Don't be afraid to go into fine detail, including adding timelines, agendas and deadlines. You are formulating a proper plan, the more detailed the better.

If, on completing the exercise, you still believe that some of your answers point to something that really is impossible for you to achieve, take another look at what you have written.

Try rewriting the answers believing that you could make this impossible thing possible. What could you genuinely do to make the impossible possible?

This is how it works when you start thinking and planning The Art of Possible. See for yourself; work on those random thoughts and find the gold in them.

"Try to do what you want to do and set the goal high. If you want it to work, why can't it? Then work hard, care and do your very best" – Jonathan Raggett, MD, Red Carnation Hotels

LIVING THE ART OF POSSIBLE

The capacity to be in the present, to be truly in the here and now, is the greatest single antidote to being held back by the past. And even more significantly it is the most powerful springboard for launching us into realising the world of the possible.

LIVE THE ART OF POSSIBLE
'RANDOM THOUGHTS CAN PROVIDE CONCRETE ANSWERS' RECAP

- You have learnt about dreaming, how to ask the right questions and the importance of being right here in the 'now';

- You have learnt to notice your daydreams, and to see if they provide you with a pattern or a signpost.

- You have learnt to look for the higher aspirations which your dreams are pointing you to.

- You have learnt to recognize what makes you feel uncomfortable. You have learnt to ask your brain the right questions, both in the present and in the context of your goals.

- You have learnt what you need to start doing today.

- You have learnt the power of being in the present moment. You have learnt to ask yourself what you can achieve today.

- You have made a plan.

CHAPTER 7

ACKNOWLEDGE YOUR STRENGTHS IN ORDER TO GROW THEM

"Genius is talent set on fire by courage" – Henry van Dyke

This chapter is about taking the time and care to acknowledge your strengths in order that they can work for you.

Whilst working with some extraordinary people from the fields of sport, the arts and business, I have noticed that they share a common trait; the ability to recognise, nurture and build their own talent.

Of course this ability to value your own strengths will be easier for some than it is for others. Yet however reluctant you are to acknowledge your own skills, it is crucial that you give yourself a chance to value your abilities.

Knowing and acknowledging your talents, and then working to build and develop them, is a powerful step towards *The Art of Possible*. Working to build on skills that you already possess encourages the brain to build the new neural pathways, as well as the new neurons, that will enable you to make your personal journey towards what is possible.

Sometimes, it is very easy to dismiss, with a throwaway remark, something that we are actually very good at with comments such as "oh, anyone can do that". Well maybe they can, but maybe they aren't doing it at this moment, or maybe they can't! The point is that right now you are the one who is doing this particular thing and what's more, you are doing it particularly well.

This chapter isn't intended to swell your head so big that you can't fit through the door. It is simply here to show you that knowing what you already have to work with makes living one's life a whole lot easier.

"If you are always trying to be normal, you will never know how amazing you can be" – Maya Angelou

Treat yourself as a project. What do you do when you start work on something new? How do you approach it?

Deepen your knowledge of yourself; recognise what you're good at, where your skills lie and what areas you shine in. Once you've done a full stock-take of your abilities you'll be in a better state of readiness for the opportunities that will pass your way. If you are in the present, in the moment, and your brain is in its receptive homeostatic state, calm but energetic, you will be open to the possibilities that lie before you. This chapter might just serve as a reminder of your talents.

Often we overlook or even forget the things that we're good at until we are reminded of them when polishing our C.V. or talking to someone about a job or new opportunity.

To define the myriad of possibilities out there for you, let's clearly define what our 'truths' are (some of which may turn out to be quite false), including who we really are or believe ourselves to be. One amazing athlete, Alison Mowbray, whilst a kid at school, was defined by others, as the 'non-sporty' sibling. So convinced was she of this truth that she carried it around for years. And yet she is now an Olympic Silver Medalist!

What outdated, outmoded or just plain untrue story do you tell about yourself to yourself, and others? How do these 'truths' affect the way you operate? Are you carrying any 'truths' or 'myths' around that need an edit? Which of these 'truths' are working for you today and which aren't? Now create some new truly truthful truths about yourself; leader, listener, inspirer, parent, teacher, sporty, energetic, entertainer, strong, motivator etc.

"Progress is impossible without change, and those who cannot change their minds cannot change anything"
— George Bernard Shaw

ART OF POSSIBLE EXPANSION EXERCISE: SO, WHO ARE YOU?

Answer the questions and write or draw a few examples. When are you at your best?

Who brings the best out in you?

What brings out the best in you, e.g. places or activities?

What are you good at?

What are you great at?

The answers that you give to these questions will give you new insight. They will serve as a reminder of your strengths and talents, and perhaps your weaknesses, which you could work on too. By the end of this exercise you will have a good idea of what you excel at and where you could iron out the rough edges.

Just the act of recognising, reliving and writing down (or drawing) this list of skills will have already strengthened the neural pathways that are the foundation stones of who you are and will pave the way to your own Art of Possible. This is particularly useful when the going gets hard.

"Strive for perfection, maximize what you have and work hard very, very hard" – Karen Atkinson MBE, England Netball

Remember, diamonds don't sparkle until they have been cut, honed, polished and held under the light. To explore this idea a little further or to give you some more ideas, consider the following:

What do people ask you to do for them?

What do people compliment you on?

What are the things that you find effortless?

What do you never get tired of?

What (and/or who) gives you energy?

You may need to research your abilities a little more by looking for further evidence of what you are good at, taking particular notice of the way in which you operate at work, at home, with friends, with family, and in all other areas of your life.

Armed with this knowledge, having strengthened the neural pathways that enable you to do what you do, you can now build on these skills. Developing your strengths will be immensely useful particularly when on a journey which encompasses change and discomfort.

Consider how you can use your attributes to achieve your greater purpose.

Feeling discomfort on a new path or journey signals that our brain is engaged in assessing our 'safe/not safe' survival response. At this point, if our talents have strong foundations it will be because we have been through this particular discomfort before. Being able to recognise this uncomfortable feeling means that we will have already developed the necessary neural pathways and will have a greater strength to move forward. In other words we will feel more comfortable in a changing, or indeed difficult situation.

Strengthening your ability to become comfortable with discomfort will make it easier to embark on what is possible for you.

"Be your own person, live your own life and achieve yourself"
— Tracey Curtis-Taylor, Aviatrix

Have you discovered anything in the answers above that you had perhaps forgotten or overlooked? Something that will help inform your goals, desires and what step you'd like to take next?

How can you use that skill or ability?

"Don't over-analyse, just try it and see what happens and constantly ask, what did you learn? In every scenario"
— Grant Allaway, MD, Ad2One Group

In identifying what brings the best out in you, be it a person, an environment or an activity like a sport, ask yourself if this motivator is a regular feature in your life, and if not, why not?

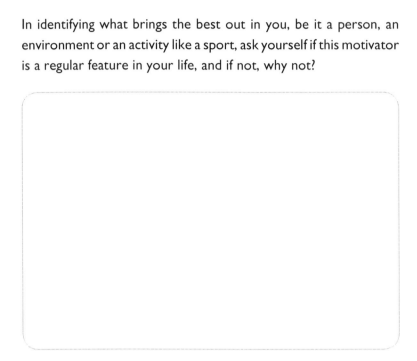

Keep these skills and talents in the front of your mind as you go through this book, and on the tougher days, refer back to it. It will serve as a little cheerleader, bolstering your spirits.

Remember your talent is the bedrock of your potential and your journey to living your own Art of Possible. Make sure you continue to recognise, acknowledge and affirm your abilities for they will serve as your greatest tools in pursuing your goals.

LIVE THE ART OF POSSIBLE 'ACKNOWLEDGE YOUR STRENGTHS TO GROW THEM' RECAP

YOU HAVE IDENTIFIED:

- What your talents are and how to know, own and fall back on these skills - they're your foundation.

- The importance of nurturing and/or developing your talents.

- Which 'truths' about you are inaccurate.

- How to make some new real 'truths'.

- What or who enables your talent to flourish.

CHAPTER 8

CURIOSITY PAYS OFF AND CAPITALISING ON LEARNING

"It is a miracle that curiosity survives formal education"
– Albert Einstein

Children are naturally curious. If you have any children in your life, yours or others, you'll be most aware that 'Why?' is one of their favourite words; from "Why can't I have a sweet?" to "Why don't the stars fall down?"

Recent neuroscience tells us that the more we can question and experience the new and the different, be it in the form of data or an activity, the better our brain can work to make possibilities real for us. This is exactly how children's brains develop and grow.

Like sponges, they soak up as much information and knowledge as they can find in order to feed their young minds. As we become adults something happens to that insatiable curiosity, either it naturally dips or perhaps it gives in to that unwritten rule in society that we should question less for fear of being seen not to know the answer. Should we really be expected to know the answer to everything or is this fear of not knowing simply something that we impose on ourselves? Of course curiosity for many does survive formal education, but it is always worth reminding ourselves to continue developing the discipline to remain curious and to keep on asking questions.

Recently I sat in a meeting at a technology company and asked how an aspect of the software worked in real terms. One of the engineers explained by way of a great drawing and then I understood. Brilliant! However, sometime later in the day, someone who was also in the meeting came up to me and said, "I'm so glad you asked that question, I had no idea of how it worked either!" He was new to the organisation, and feeling that he should know how the thing worked, hadn't dared to ask for an explanation, and so he kept himself in the dark. Asking a question, and other forms of data seeking, are rarely a 'bad' way to go about things. And more often than not we will discover that we are far from the 'only' person who wanted to know the answer.

As we have learned, asking questions and gaining new information strengthens our brains into being 'comfortable with discomfort'. In other words, asking a question when we think we should know the answer can cause discomfort, but when we get an answer, and with it new sources of information, we can move forward.

If, as adults, we become less interested in new things, we will find that this absence of stimulation is likely to make our lives feel smaller and less enriched. Rather than suffer this fate, how much better to ask what we could gain by once more developing the discipline to be more curious?

New knowledge, new experiences, new people and new places invariably take us on a journey of learning, knowledge and enrichment. And it is during this journey that we get closer to living *The Art of Possible*.

I've heard folk say that research is "formalised curiosity"and others claim that it is 'nosiness' — either way, the desire to know more broadens the mind, expands our knowledge, provides learning and is always stimulating. And an excuse to be just a bit nosy is quite appealing too!

ART OF POSSIBLE EXPANSION EXERCISE

To develop your own curiosity and interest, consider the following questions:

Think about how you feel when you are really curious, intrigued or interested by something.

What piques your interest?

What makes you curious?

Who intrigues you?

Your curiosity may be the most subtle of feelings, you may not even know why it is there, but this matters not. What is important is the noticing and being aware of the moment.

Now, think about your goals and dreams:

What aspects of your dreams make you curious or excited?

Think of a role model or someone who inspires you – what is it about them that you find so stimulating? What else would you love to know about them?

When you have made an unfavourable assumption about someone, curiosity can be a very helpful way of shifting yourself away from being judgemental and into a more inquisitive mode. Another way of making your brain comfortable with discomfort.

Next time you have an uncharitable thought about someone or something, remember your curiosity:

Ask them a question.

About anything!

Your surroundings, the weather, (where would conversation be without the weather!)

If you're at an event, ask who they're connected to or why they are attending.

If you are making an assumption about a stranger, try suspending judgement for a moment to ask whether the opposite to your judgement couldn't also be true.

A client of mine, a senior manager, mentioned that he had a challenging and sometimes argumentative relationship with a member of staff. However, one day he came to me with a revelation about this colleague who had previously so annoyed him. He had happened to overhear another member of the team talking about how successful this person had been in their chosen sport. It was the very same sport that my client most enjoyed, and so, in the spirit of trying to build a better relationship, he decided to strike up a conversation about it with his colleague. It transpired that indeed they had a shared passion. Sparks still fly between them but their relationship has been transformed by their discovery of a common bond. Simple curiosity and a willingness to ask more meant that they could move their communication on to a better place.

When you exercise your curiosity and deepen your interest, the world becomes bigger, your insight broader, and brain plasticity develops too.

What's the worst that might happen if you allow yourself to be curious? If you ask someone a question and they don't grant you an answer, or the person you gave a second chance to confirms that your original assessment of them was correct, it's simply time to move on. Nothing ventured, nothing gained. Remember that you are on a journey and there are plenty more people in the world for you to find fascinating.

Work your curiosity like a muscle… you never know who you might end up meeting, what you might find out, or what opportunities you might uncover. Curiosity will motivate your brain to learn and be more flexible – and hurrah to that!

Feed your brain.

Another brilliant asset our brain has is its plasticity. Brain plasticity is essentially the extraordinary ability of the brain to modify its own structure and function, following changes within the body or in the external environment, as well as in our experiences, by building new connections. The more we engage our curiosity and keep our brain nimble, the more knowledge and experience we have to enable us to live *The Art of Possible*.

By exposing ourselves to the 'new', the brain's dynamic response to difference and the ability to change our behaviour and actions will create new neurons and access all areas – like a VIP pass.

Broadening your interests will make you more innovative. And innovation signifies that your brain is searching for connections and stimulation, firing more neurons, which in turn strengthen the axons (the little wires) that fortify the pathways in our brains which develop the plasticity.

Our brains have evolved to learn, but they perform best when the learning is demanding. When we learn new, challenging 'stuff' really exercising our brain, it will reward us by firing clearer, faster signals. As an added bonus, this cognitive exercising will also stop existing neurons from wasting away or degrading.

Keep on feeding your brain, rewarding it with new challenges, new input, so that it can get to work on making new connections. Give as much difference or new stuff to your brain as you possibly can. It will power your thinking and your possibilities!

"The best thing you can do is to find the thing that you're not interested in; that is where there is a hole in our knowledge and we're blind to it" – Araceli Camargo, Neuroscientist

ART OF POSSIBLE EXPANSION EXERCISE

Build your curiosity to develop your plasticity.

This might seem like a very odd suggestion. Can you identify what you are NOT interested in?

*
*
*
*

Now go and search for it! Go to a lecture on it, go to a sports fixture, change your usual routine. The list is endless...

*

*

*

*

*

"Education is something that takes a person to another level"
– Ashok Vaswani, CEO Corporate and Personal Banking, Barclays

As we've discovered, plasticity will help develop and grow your brain. However, there is something else that you will need to consider in order to realise your brain's true potential, and that is what other kind of fuel beyond stimulation are you offering it?

Matron-like as it may sound, living *The Art of Possible* will also mean feeding your body with food that nourishes the brain. Ask yourself honestly, "am I getting enough water, physical exercise and sleep to think properly?" Without adequate amounts of these key components your brain simply won't be able to function at its best.

So take a look at the requirements below and be prepared to ask yourself if you need to embrace 'difference' here too, and make a change to your diet, your exercise regime or your sleep patterns in order to optimise your brain power.

Nutrition: the brain loves the following foods: sodium, aka salt (but opt for natural sources of salt such as beetroot, celery, meat, spinach etc.); magnesium (green leafy vegetables, nuts, fish, bananas, beans and whole grains etc.); zinc (shellfish, sesame and pumpkin seeds, cheese, lamb etc.) and potassium (beans, green leafy vegetables, potatoes, fish, bananas and avocados etc.)

Feed your brain as much fresh and/or freshly prepared food as is possible. Omega 3 from oily fish is particularly fab for the brain as well as for the skin and the joints.

Get regular exercise: hard cardiovascular exercise, the kind that gets you out of breath is the best – when we exert ourselves in this way the brain's frontal lobe is flooded with dopamine, a type of neurotransmitter which helps us to think.

Water: drink lots and lots of it. It's easier than you think to become dehydrated. I know one very fit, healthy person who didn't drink enough during a particularly hot summers day and wound up in hospital. Dehydration is bad news all round; bad for the body and bad for the brain.

Dehydration causes a lack of vigilance, some difficulty in performing mental tasks and problems with our working memory. And take note that these symptoms were the result of many studies of those with a more sedentary work and home environment, rather than those with an active lifestyle.

To demonstrate the point further, I will tell you the story of when I went to interview an extraordinary female aviator in an airfield in the south of England in freezing, rather than naturally dehydrating conditions.

I was out on the airfield when I had a call of nature and ventured into the fire station to find a loo. Once there, a poster caught my eye: "Are you hydrated enough?" ran the strapline, followed by a chart of colours from palest yellow to dark yellowy-brown, and against each colour was written the description of the levels of hydration it indicated. The chart explained that if your urine was darker than a certain shade of yellow you were in need of water in order to rehydrate. However, what I noticed most were the words written against the darkest shade of yellow at the bottom of the chart. YOU SHOULDN'T BE FLYING! rang out the warning, You will be a danger to yourself and others!

From a conversation later in the day, I know that our team and the film crew all used the services of the fire station, and were inspired to have an extra glass of water whilst there too! It was a powerful wake-up call to the serious effects of dehydration on our brain's power to function.

Good Sleep: much of our subconscious thinking happens when we are asleep and this is where much of the transformative thought and innovation comes from. There is much research out there about the importance and power of sleep and, less pleasantly, the use of sleep-depravation in torture situations, which horribly demonstrates how crucial sleep is for our bodies and minds. Sleep also plays a very important role in learning – it helps cement the new knowledge that we're taking in, making it all the easier to recall at a later date. Beware the regular 'all-nighters' – okay every now and again – however, recent research suggests that if you don't sleep enough, your ability to learn could drop by as much as forty per cent!

LIVE THE ART OF POSSIBLE 'CURIOSITY PAYS OFF AND CAPITALISING ON LEARNING' RECAP

YOU HAVE LEARNT AND BEEN CURIOUS ABOUT:

- What you have been curious about today and what you should do about feeding this curiosity.

- What you are curious about when you think about your goals.

- What you are 'not' interested in... and how learning about it can present you with a real opportunity to find out something new (even if it doesn't immediately appeal).

- What you have learned today.

- Whether you have met anyone new this week.

- The importance of eating well, hydrating well and sleeping well.

CHAPTER 9

USE YOUR TALENTS TO GET UNSTUCK

Raw talent; your mind is amazingly flexible and agile, though you may not always realise it.

It is our strengths and talents that power our potential and what's possible for us. Our talent is hugely valuable to us yet sometimes we neither see it nor recognise it. When working in an industry of people who have similar skills to us, all of us will have a point of difference from one another, a particular talent that the others don't have. Finding this 'sweet spot' of yours is a great exercise for you to have a go at. It is so very much easier to play to our strengths, than to try to improve the skills that we have to work harder at because they don't come so naturally to us.

Play to your strengths and back your weaknesses, as a mentor very early in my career once commented.

"Everyone has talent. What is rare is the courage to follow the talent to the place where it leads" – Erica Jong

It is almost impossible for our brain to be innovative when it is in fight or flight mode, or when we are too stressed, anxious or fixed in our thinking to make way for productive thoughts.

As you'll know when you start using your gifts and talents to earn a living, you will naturally gravitate towards the type of work that you have a natural aptitude for and can even excel at. But there's more. As Walt Disney said, "It's kind of fun to do the impossible".

"Profit is a by-product of doing something well" – Anthony Thomson, Atom Bank

There is a whole other higher level of amazing that we could allow ourselves to be, yet most of us are blind to our potential. We tend to judge our ability on what we believe ourselves (truly or mistakenly) to be capable of today and in the future. Our perception of our own abilities may be based in reality or in myth, but so often these abilities are blocked, either by our own, or by other negative beliefs, that we find ourselves unable to push through these levels of discomfort to reach our true capabilities.

Back to homeostasis – remember deep thinking requires a calm, still mind. Big ideas, big changes and big solutions need to be considered when your mind is in a balanced place of calm and energy. Provided your friends, family or colleagues aren't in danger – **and there isn't a bear to fight** – work on restoring yourself to that place of homeostasis as soon as possible.

ART OF POSSIBLE EXPANSION EXERCISE

Consider all your strengths; which of them would you like to become really great at doing or being?

Is there a talent that you can hone further which will run like a gold thread through everything you do?

Could there be a talent inside you that you don't yet know, lying dormant, waiting for you to notice it?

Everyone has natural gifts and talents, yet they can so easily remain unrealised or even undiscovered. As previously mentioned, rowing champion Alison Mowbray didn't come to rowing until she was 18 after a somewhat non-sporty childhood. It was purely by chance that she discovered she had a natural aptitude for rowing after a University friend asked her to come rowing with her one cold morning. Alison said, why not? Only to realise, once she was on the water with the oars in her hands, that she had found her purpose. The rest is history, for Alison went on to become an Olympic silver medalist for Great Britain in quadruple sculls in Athens in 2004.

Make a conscious decision to nurture, develop and hone an existing talent that you know you already have. Be disciplined too in developing your other habits and then build some time into your schedule, at least once a month, to do something new. A new activity, something unfamiliar, especially in an area completely outside your existing range of interests, even one you feel might bore you. Challenging your brain in this way is a great way to start swimming in the deeper, initially uncomfortable, waters of what you might be capable of.

It is more than likely that whilst exploring these new areas in your life, something really interesting might lead your curiosity to want to explore it in further depth.

Ask yourself what your existing natural gifts and talents are and which of these you'd like to hone and develop in the next few years?

Now ask yourself what you are gifted at:

Have you the courage to fulfil its promise?

How can you prioritise some time to develop it?

Perhaps there is something that you are naturally gifted at but which remains undiscovered deep inside you, something you need to set to work on excavating. Begin your hunt for your undiscovered talents by setting aside time each week to try out new experiences, exploring how you respond to new possibilities. Don't turn down opportunities or invitations to do something just because the idea makes you feel uncomfortable, unless of course it is genuinely dangerous. It is important to keep the momentum going as you seek out new and different experiences. Make sure you explore as broadly as possible – your latest pursuit may not be something that you decide to carry on with forever, but it is more than likely to be right for you in this moment – simply because it is still a novelty. Where will you start?

"Find out what you get excited about and do something about it" – Ashok Vaswani, CEO, Personal & Corporate Banking, Barclays

What are you truly capable of?

Sometimes people use difficulties, real or imaginary, as an excuse not to fulfil their potential, and to remain living a half-lived life. The sad fact is that most of us choose to use only a very small percentage of our capabilities. A common misconception I hear amongst people who are struggling to live *The Art of Possible* is that they are at a disadvantage. They use their belief that others 'have it easier', 'are more naturally talented' than they are, 'have had more opportunities in life', 'haven't been through what they have been through', …. and so the list goes on. Regardless of whether these complaints are based in fact or not, the fact remains that focusing on unfavourably comparing one's life to another's won't take anyone nearer to their own goals or to help them live *The Art of Possible*.

At the same time as we are fully utilising our talents, we might also be working on coping with or getting over hardship. Indeed our desire to live *The Art of Possible* may well have been sparked by a difficulty, whether recent or in the past.

Everyone has to face difficulties in their lives to a greater or lesser degree; a heartache, tragedy, relationship breakdown, illness, bereavement, a hard upbringing, a career disaster, a poor education… the list of challenges that life can throw at us is endless.

Sometimes we let our difficulties define us. Each of us is a remarkable being with remarkable potential, yet it is often true that up to this point we may not have been choosing to live our best life. If we can recognise that whatever has happened in our life so far has made us who we are, we will be able to choose between using our life experiences as a brilliant foundation rather than allowing it to keep us stuck.

Are you staying in your comfort zone, or, to put it more accurately, your 'comfort trap'?

Some people stay anchored to a low point in their lives, finding comfort or safety in the fact that they never dare to venture beyond this 'comfort' zone into discomfort. Others choose to stay connected to a high point in their past, often referring back to it and never getting beyond it. Identifying oneself solely with past events, either the highs or the lows, will keep one stuck to these events, unable to move forward.

When we set our minds in this rigid way we find it far harder to live in the present or progress our lives forward. Blinkering ourselves like this limits our ability to actually see the possibilities standing in front of our eyes. Whatever the difficulties that you have faced, (be they problems that you are currently experiencing, experienced long ago or experience intermittently), it is important to gain control over them. This is done by changing the way you think about them so that they don't disable you from being open to new ideas and stimuli, or stop you from becoming comfortable with discomfort.

"Moving away from anxiety gives you extra space for working memory and higher thinking" – Araceli Camargo

Another misconception we often share is that other people are more 'sorted' and tough than we are.

However people might appear to be on surface level, it's dangerous to make assumptions about how things are for them, particularly if we use those assumptions to hold ourselves back. Instead we can choose to focus on being gentler on ourselves, appreciating our own talents and abilities and giving ourselves permission to move forward.

And we can extend this generosity of spirit to others. As Richard Attenborough once said:

"Always treat people with kindness, everyone has a battle of some sort going on, big or small"

If you think someone is 'normal', i.e has an easy life with no difficulty in it, then the chances are you probably don't know them very well!

NEW HABITS

The best antidote to the past is to be in the present and to develop new habits.

The human condition means experiencing, both positively and negatively, a wide spectrum of life events. The spectrum of human successes and tragedies incorporating joy, heartache and breathtaking 'miraculous' moments are the wonders of life.

To make a mistake is also to be human. We may choose to wallow in regret or despair but at some point or another, when we want to go for something new or different, or just experience a shift in our lives, we will have to carry ourselves forward. We need to learn to forgive ourselves, to forgive others and to move on.

Humans are creatures of habit, we like things to be the same. Change is typically difficult for us humans which explains why we are so good at resisting it!

Change is hard because generally it causes us stress. When a stressful situation occurs (a hole appears in your finances, an emergency happens, a relationship breaks down, time pressure bears down on you, your workload mounts or any of the other millions of anxiety-making possibilities takes place), the stress hormones adrenaline and cortisol get to work, 'waking us up' from the calm and energetic, homeostatic state to deal with a given situation. Adrenaline and cortisol exist to get us ready to either fight or flee. This 'triggered state' worked well for Neanderthal man or woman, when threats to their safety were both real and fairly constant, and of course they are helpful if you've inadvertently wandered into the path of danger and you need to hotfoot it out of the way. However, if we remain in a prolonged state of constantly heightened adrenaline and cortisol it can have an unhealthy effect on our lives. Sometimes very unhealthy.

When worry and anxiety start 'looping', causing us to constantly think about the 'what ifs' and perhaps even 'catastrophizing', then our talent and potential are compromised. If you wake up worried in the middle of the night and continue worrying throughout the day, your brain becomes so cluttered with fear that your working memory is impaired. Not surprisingly under these conditions your ability to have an 'aha!' moment, or indeed just a good idea, is severely limited, at best. At worst, you will begin to experience debilitating depression.

However stress isn't always a bad emotion to experience; indeed when it is handled efficiently it can actually be good for us. When the stress we experience is not enough to cause us undue fear or excitement (for example when we encounter a change in circumstances which is not life-threatening), we should be able to use it to sharpen our wits.

If whilst experiencing stress we can get back to our own place of calm and energetic homeostasis, our response to stress can be phenomenally powerful. If we allow our brain to become calm (yet energetic) enough to make considered and often inspired decisions it will be able to take us forward, rather than telling us to either run away or get into a fight.

If you think you may be experiencing depression, do seek help from a GP, CBT therapist or specialist as soon as possible. It is a serious condition and it is good to get help sooner rather than later.

Now is the time to refer back to your plan, and if any of it seems a bit hard (or perhaps scary), considering the following points will help you to work through each change and action.

You may already have a tried and tested technique for getting back to a place of clearer, calmer thinking, but if not, try the following:

Breathe deeply – the brain needs oxygen for higher thinking. In and out, three or four deep breaths at a time whilst you try to just focus on the depth and intake of your breath.

Stand up, if you can; you'll get more oxygen.

An amazing former dancer that I know does what she calls a body audit. Whilst she's taking those deep breaths, she literally focuses her attention on each part of her body all the way from the tip of her toes, up her shins to her knees, thighs, pelvis, hips, tummy, lungs, heart, fingertips, elbows, arms, shoulders, neck, jawline, head, nose, eyes, then her ears until she reaches the top of her head. Just this small action gets her closer to becoming less stressed and more alert. I started using this technique too some time ago and I know that it works.

It is a simple action that all of us can do whenever we feel the need. It will help us to reach that calm place, one that is backed up by neuroscience, a technique that will enable us to think and act more effectively. Obviously, some of you may be thinking "well alcohol, or even drugs, could achieve the same effect", but in the stakes of training your brain, neither of these 'solutions' are a good idea. And besides, this relaxation exercise is completely free.

Breathing deeply supplies oxygen to the brain, and drinking a glass of water will also help because it will rehydrate us and refuel the brain. Drinking water also flushes out the toxins that will have been released through the stress, heightened adrenaline and cortisol.

In fact just by writing about this relaxation exercise has caused my breathing to slow and my shoulders have dropped and relaxed. Why don't you have a go too?

Of course relaxing your way back into homeostasis won't solve your immediate predicament, but it will help you to become sufficiently calm to be able to think clearly about what is causing you stress, and even find a solution.

Then ask yourself one question, in the moment:

What is the first step to take your
talent to a higher level and find a solution?

The great news is that this first step is probably a very simple one.

LIVE THE ART OF POSSIBLE 'USE YOUR TALENTS TO GET UNSTUCK' RECAP

YOU HAVE LEARNT:

- It's fun to do the impossible.

- To look for any difficulties from the past (or present) which might be keeping you stuck.

- What your talents are.

- To ask yourself when was the last time you developed your talents.

- To seek out new experiences, activities, people and things that excite you.

- To acknowledge and embrace the discomfort of change, because it will ultimately take you to a more comfortable place.

- To breathe, relax and rehydrate.

- To respond to stress in a calm yet energetic way.

CHAPTER 10

PAYING ATTENTION TO SMALL DETAILS PAYS OFF

"Be ruthless in your preparation and pay attention to every detail. Leave nothing to chance and then you can be completely in the moment" – Karen Atkinson MBE, England Netball

When we pay attention to all the little details, very often the big details take care of themselves. When we are looking at that big idea, seeking out the possibilities and new opportunities in our lives, it is the little things that we do which will pave the way.

As we've discussed before, taking care of the big stuff can seem onerous or even impossible. Breaking the task into small steps makes it more manageable, whilst paying attention to the other details in your life (from ensuring that you meet regular work deadlines, monitoring customer feedback to keeping tabs on budgets and expenditure) will pave the way to your success.

Forgetting 'little' things (which if left unattended can turn into big things) can cause unnecessary stress or just lead to inefficient use of your time.

All the successful people who I've worked with and interviewed pay great attention to all the details that might make a difference to their performance, product, experience or service.

For example, a client who runs a chain of boutiques espouses the maxim, "You never get a second chance to make a first impression". The level of detail she affords to every aspect of her business is superb. Not a thing is overlooked, from how her boutique looks at opening time (spotless, neat and welcoming) to the quality of the coffee served. All of these details constitute the finer points of her big goals, which are to open two more boutiques in the UK in the next 24 months and one in Lisbon.

ART OF POSSIBLE EXPANSION EXERCISE

Have you paid attention to all the details associated with your goals?

If your goal is to run a marathon, your first step will be to pay attention to your condition, i.e. how fit you are now, how fit you need to be, how you will find time to train, what kit you will need for training etc.

So having identified your goal, write a list of the steps, including the fine details, that will take you from where you are now to where you want to be.

Do you know what the smaller details are? It could be finance expertise, knowing the numbers, understanding how to balance profit and loss, checking that your messaging is 'on brand' every time.

Ask yourself a few questions about the details you might need to consider. For example, if your goal is to get a promotion, what skills could you learn or brush up on; i.e. presentation or managing teams?

Equally important, you might also consider your impact upon others.

As much as you are the driver to the next phase of your life, the people around you will play a part too, albeit to a greater or lesser degree. So paying attention to people and behaviours will be just as important as paying attention to the tactical and strategic details.

Some will wholeheartedly support you, others very much less so. Who are the people most close to you that it may impact upon?

Do you notice the behaviours around you, the good, the less good and the downright ugly?

Have you considered what might be causing people to behave in this way?

What image or behaviour are you projecting; for example self-assuredness about your goals or hesitancy and lack of confidence?

Does your attitude bring out the best out in others?

Does it impact, inspire, draw people in or repel them?

In order to explore and identify the details that are important for you with more clarity, I want you to look at your big goals again.

Allow yourself to gain more knowledge and insight about your goals and how you will successfully achieve them by stepping outside your own shoes and acting as if your goals belong to someone else. What do you now notice about your objectives having looked at them from a distance? Have any details been overlooked?

Are any details missing? You might discover glaring omissions, because sometimes we can get so absorbed in our own stuff that we miss obvious things. This is why just the act of stepping back and pretending that the goal belongs to someone else can reveal so much for you.

What advice would you give someone else about how to achieve this goal?

What would you observe?

Once you have done this and really excavated deep into your goals, you may well discover gems of information, which will considerably enrich your goal strategy or action plan.

LIVING THE ART OF POSSIBLE

One of my clients, the charismatic CEO of a FTSE 250 company, always concerns himself with five daily goals, which are already part of the overall company strategy. He encourages each of his team members to apply the same rule. It maintains focus and serves the business well. Paying attention to five details at a time ensures that every element of company strategy and vision is paid attention to and five is a good number for the brain to hang onto. More than that and we don't hold sufficient detail. This system keeps him and his teams focused and perhaps even more importantly, allows the company the freedom to question, challenge or rewrite and do things differently, simply because the overall goal has been broken down into component parts which are therefore easier to work with.

This attention to detail has become a daily company discipline and therefore an individual discipline and habit too.

"When I want something, I go for it and I ensure that everything that is within my control is exactly that; the car, the power delivery, my physical fitness, every detail"
– Robb Gravett, Former British Touring Car Champion

The difference between something good and something amazing usually lies in the attention to detail.

LIVE THE ART OF POSSIBLE 'ATTENTION TO DETAIL PAYS OFF' RECAP

YOU HAVE LEARNT:

- How to explore every detail associated with your goals.

- Whether you are paying attention to the deeper stuff as well as the surface details.

- Whether your big goal inspires others and why.

- Whether you need to learn a new skill or implement a new system.

- That acting as if your goals are someone else's helps you gain insight into what you want to achieve.

- To really pay attention to every last detail.

PART 3

USING DIFFICULTY

CHAPTER 11

SHAKE OFF DOUBTS

When we strike out beyond where we've never been before, we may well be alone and in need of internal strength. Or we may need to rally our supporters so that they can help us face the discomfort ahead.

There are those who will have your best interests at heart, and those who unfortunately won't, so sorting out the supporters from the opponents early on will help smooth your path to success.

"If you suffer from a lack of self-esteem or low confidence, it may be that you're surrounded by a***holes" – Anon

We all need supporters, helpers and cheerleaders from time to time. Okay, they may not have the pom-poms, but a sincere, well-timed hug or positive comment from someone who cares, is worth a million 'going-through-the-motions' grand gestures. These allies are invaluable when the going is easy, and will be even more of an asset when the going gets hard. Take the time to identify who these people are and to recognise how they can help you along your journey – from boosting you with the odd text of support or taking care of one of your responsibilities, to mentoring you or teaching you a skill.

Given that we can be easily brought down or lifted up by the people around us, it is crucial that we choose the right support team.

But beware, there are 'theys' who could serve to diminish our resolve or worse stop us in our tracks.

Do you sometimes find yourself held back in some way when thinking about, or even blaming, an unknown yet powerful group of 'frenemies' who are judging your every move?

Or do you have very real people around you who freely give you negative feedback about what you are attempting.

The group whose judgements we imagine, are sometimes the often automatic product of our subconscious mind. Everyone's 'they' differs. It could be society or family, colleagues or an individual, or even 'it' crowd. In our heads, we can replay their opinions, worrying about their reaction and measuring ourselves against the standard we believe they set.

The 'they' that we carry in our minds may be solely about our fears and perceptions, or they may be rooted in reality.

We are holding ourselves back when we worry about what these people are thinking about our efforts to reach our goal.

Figuring out who to turn to for support when we feel worried about taking a particular course of action is crucial. If we choose to listen to our cheerleaders, including our own rallying thoughts, we will be bolstering our courage and bravery to do whatever it is that we really want to do.

But if we choose to focus on the negatives we may well end up distracted and dismayed.

Have a think about who 'they' might be in your life? You may not be consciously aware of who they are. You may be surprised! Are 'they' your colleagues, family, friends or maybe your community, or even society as a whole. Are you perhaps held back by what 'other people' think of you, or what you think they think of you?

WARNING: 'They' can be a powerful bunch.

'They' may well tell you quite categorically what they consider you mustn't, shouldn't, oughtn't or couldn't do. Their naysaying will often be presented as being in your best interests, whereas in the majority of cases they are transferring their insecurities, rather than yours, onto you.

These negative frenemies might be family or friends, who, deliberately or out of habit, try to hold you back, often cloaking their criticism as 'concerned advice' or 'in your best interest'. This negativity will feel most unpleasant, sometimes hurtful or even heart-wrenching.

It is a harsh reality that some people will feel very uncomfortable about you changing and working towards your passions and a changed life, and will project their discomfort onto you quite strongly. Sadly, people will fall away, but new friends will arrive in time. This too is part of the discomfort (and excitement) of meeting new experiences and people during the journey.

When I undertook the challenge to ride over the Pyrenees there were friends and family who told me, in no uncertain terms, that I was thoughtless and irresponsible to be attempting such a thing, and that I should cancel the whole trip.

Motorbikes can be dangerous, as can mountains, and I was someone with responsibilities – perhaps that was their reasoning. As I see it, life is full of dangers anyway; in the home, in the garden, on the road. I was not driven by lust for danger, but by the desire to do something that challenged me, and more importantly, would raise money for two wonderful children's charities who had helped our daughter enormously when she was poorly.

The discomfort and anxiety that others can project into our lives is immense. However, it is important to recognise that you have a choice as to how to react. You can choose to feel overwhelmed and hurt, or you can instead choose to feel strong and motivated despite what is going on, or being said, around you. I'm not suggesting it is easy; it isn't, but you can do it.

When at the receiving end of negative 'advice', I turned to my supportive friends, and it was their encouragement and support which made the destructive comments easier to deflect. Sure the comments from the critical 'theys' were still hurtful but they weren't enough to stop me in my tracks. Above all I knew why I was doing what I was doing, and more to the point, that I was determined to do it. While that may sound a little self-centred, the fact is that to be resolved to do something requires a degree of inner strength. And if it flickers from time to time, there are always external sources who can protect us from our ambitions being blown out altogether.

If you find that your mind is full of critical voices, ask yourself which positive encouragers you could train your brain to think of instead? Who are the people in your life who support you unconditionally, who would willingly push you forward towards your dreams – who'd help strengthen your ability to cope with the discomfort?

ART OF POSSIBLE EXPANSION EXERCISE

Consider those who support you wholeheartedly.

When the positive power of ' they' appears, consider what 'they' can do to help you reach your goals? A kind word or conversation with a colleague or friend, a feel-good movie, taking a walk or strenuous exercise together. Think deeply about what will work for you.

*

*

*

*

"It takes a great deal of bravery to stand up to our enemies, but just as much to stand up to our friends" – JK Rowling

Remember earlier when we talked about how becoming more comfortable with discomfort strengthens your neural pathways and creates new neurons? Well standing up to the doubters and striding out on your determined path has the same brain-building effect.

Going against the grain of perceived wisdom to follow your own dream will be hard and uncomfortable. Some of the cheerleaders might disappear, whilst the critical will likely be quite vocal. It's best to accept now that encountering discouragement is an inevitable part of the journey to living your own Art of Possible.

At this point, being courageous enough to be different, and focusing on giving your brain new and different data, will help develop the muscle of potential and possibility. And give you the strength to develop armour that will protect you from the doubters.

Remember that you have a choice as to how to live your life; to either follow a path that someone else has drawn for you or to set out on your own journey. If you are brave enough to choose your own path you will soon find yourself accompanied by supporters who you didn't even know existed.

There will always be naysayers.

Try to ignore them, there are plenty of them and they will always be there, at times even growing in number.

Yet it's true that 'they' can have a phenomenally paralysing effect on what you want to do, unless you work at wrestling your life back out of their hands, and their heads.

"Do not go where the path may lead, go instead where there is no path and leave a trail" – Ralph Waldo Emerson

There will always be plenty of people to say, "But that won't work!"

The punchy founder of a funky drinks company has a great observation about how to build effective teams:

"You must review regularly and promote, delegate or terminate"

This may sound a little harsh perhaps and presents obvious problems when applied to family, but the fact remains that those who bring us down, rather than help us up, are never going to be particularly supportive or nourishing people to have around, especially when the going gets tough.

"It's better to be alone than in bad company" – George Washington

Think about all those around you who will consider your aspirations, support your belief and ambitions, nurture, teach and metaphorically or physically hold your hand along the way.

Now go back to Chapter 3 and next to each of those big goals you noted, write down two reasons as to why you believe they will work, reinforcing that power within you.

Of course there will be obstacles and hurdles to overcome but dwelling on them won't move you forward. Focus on what you can do, what you've done before, what you know that you can do and in doing so diminish the power of the doubters.

LIVING THE ART OF POSSIBLE

If you think you don't have enough time, remember that you have exactly the same number of hours per day as Helen Keller, Maya Angelou, Louis Pasteur, Michelangelo, Steve Jobs, Larry Page, Sergey Brin, JK Rowling, Adele, Lewis Hamilton, Valentino Rossi , Usain Bolt and, and, and

ART OF POSSIBLE EXPANSION EXERCISE

Now list six people who can help you achieve your goals and dreams, including those who will give you constructive and even hard feedback. They might be able to teach you something, inspire you, introduce you to someone helpful or just make you feel plain good about yourself – which in itself is priceless.

1

2

3

4

5

6

List six people who make you happy and/or support you (your cheerleaders).

It could be your partner, your boss, someone else's boss, your heroes (childhood or current), someone in the public eye, your friend, your child, someone else's child, someone you work with, or even the barista who makes your coffee just the way you like it. These are the people to call, text, or (particularly in the case of the people you know less well) just think about when you are having a hard day.

1

2

3

4

5

6

"We rarely remember exactly what someone said or exactly what someone did, but we always remember how they made us feel" – Anon

When I was learning to ride an off-road motorbike, I found it, as you will have read, extremely difficult. One day when I was in the middle of a forest in Wales, really struggling with my bike and not keeping up with the group, the "what am I doing here" type of thoughts started coming thick and fast. Suddenly a handsome chap appeared from nowhere, rode past, then turned and rode side-saddle (very impressive) and yelled "You can do it, girl!", grinned and sped off again. Just thinking about that moment whenever I need to has taken me through many, many hard days. It made me smile, still does, because not only did it break my despondent mood, but I also managed to do as he predicted and succeed.

If you are ready to move on, brilliant. If you are still wavering a little about whether you are able to face this new scary thing, this big challenge that feels quite impossible right now, the real question you need to ask yourself is:

"Well, why not me?"

A Fortune 100 CFO said to me during a session, "When I've told you about my ambitions, you have never once asked 'Why?'. Always, 'Well why not, why not you?'"

That question, "Well why not you?" lies at the heart of my coaching style because it is one of the keys to living *The Art of Possible*. You don't need to wait to be chosen or approved of by 'they'; you don't need perfect conditions or to be 100% experienced and skilled, you just need to ask why on earth not?

So here too, I'm asking you. Yes, you!

Why not you?

If not you, then it will be someone else who will live your idea of what is possible, someone else who will follow your dream, make it real and blaze your trail, so why not get there before they do? Start today. You have your goals. Your cheerleaders are there, supporting you, who even on the tough days will more than compensate for the doubters, fending off the debilitating effects of what the naysayers are saying.

LIVE THE ART OF POSSIBLE
'SHAKE OFF THE DOUBTS' RECAP

- You have considered and powered your mental strength.

- You have looked to see if you are being held back by an unknown yet powerful 'frenemy'.

- You have identified your supporters, teachers, mentors and cheerleaders and listed them.

- You have learned how to strengthen your muscle of potential and develop and elevated your thinking to block out the doubts.

- You have asked, "Why not me?"

- You have identified what you are going to progress with today with the help of your supporters.

CHAPTER 12

RESILIENCE WHEN THE GOING IS HARD

RIDING THROUGH THE DIFFICULT TIMES

There are some days when the going will be tough, even painful. We are emotional beings, and are naturally stirred or emotionally affected by all sorts of things, feelings that we often can't avoid.

We might be affected by tragedies close to home, or dreadful events happening further afield to people we don't know. The situations we find ourselves in might be of our own or others' making, and might range from relationship difficulties or illness to physical or mental challenges or financial troubles, and of course a myriad of other things.

All these life events can have an impact on how we deal with challenges. On these difficult days, our best course is to acknowledge how we feel and then move ahead, even if it's just a very small bit. While realizing that being resilient is sometimes easier said than done,

It's nonetheless what must be done. A smart businesswoman remarked to me recently that people don't drown from falling in the water, they drown from staying there. So, whatever the predicament is that we find ourselves in, at some point we just need to act and take a step forward.

HOW TO TACKLE LET-DOWNS AND DEVELOP RESILIENCE

"The worst thing that you can do in life is to not have a go. If you fail, it doesn't matter, you pick yourself up, dust yourself down and start again" – Rick Parry, Former CEO and Chairman of Liverpool FC

Let-downs, obstacles and the unexpected are all part of life's journey. It is our attitude to these drawbacks and how we deal with them that will either positively or negatively impact on our way forward. Our attitude in these situations is what will distinguish those of us who embrace living *The Art of Possible* from those who don't.

It can be easy to inadvertently make things worse for yourself by reacting in a way that discourages you further. Successful people living *The Art of Possible* have learned to turn difficult things to their advantage.

Responding in an overly emotional or dramatic way to something can simply draw more attention to ourselves when we least want it. If our reaction to the frustration, fear or angst we are experiencing overrides or is different from our usual behaviour, then people will begin to notice and have their own emotional response. In other words we need to take care that our response doesn't impact unfavourably on those around us.

When we're feeling stuck, hurt or unable to do something, we tend to metaphorically, or sometimes even physically, make ourselves smaller; in our voice, posture and general way of being. Sometimes this closing in on ourselves is done subconsciously. We feel uncomfortable, so our brain's protective survival mechanism kicks in, that 'safe or not safe?' analysing of information. At this stage if we are not comfortable (enough) with the discomfort we are most likely to respond to the 'not safe' that we find ourselves in, and will take ourselves back to our comfort zone. At some point we just need to override, act and take a step forward.

ART OF POSSIBLE EXPANSION EXERCISE

Remember this simple exercise? Stand tall, lift both your voice and your head up. These actions can't take the pain, fear or concern away but they will change your position, literally as well as neurologically.

When we stand tall, we are perceived to be in control, confident and alert. We may not feel any of those things but to the outside world, this is how we look and people will treat us accordingly. Remember how unreliable it is to form an opinion on people based on how they appear.

If we were lost in a new place, we'd ask directions of someone who looks like they know where they are, not someone who also looks lost!

When you present yourself in this way and people begin treating you as someone who is composed and self-assured, you may well start to feel better. And as your mood improves, so more importantly, will your belief that you do actually have some control or influence on the situation. The pain won't have gone but you may have managed to shift how you feel about it.

Try it and see.

When something hard happens or you are challenged uncomfortably, shift your posture away from appearing vulnerable, defensive or frightened to one of being resolute and strong. You may very well not feel anything of the kind, but that doesn't matter, the fact is that just having the appearance of someone who is strong will make all the difference.

We can either accept life events and learn from them or let them pull us down.

"Tomorrow is another day" – Hoda M Ali, FGM/C survivor and campaigner

Very often the hardest things to bear will be the ones that we learn the most from, even though it may feel unendurably tough at the time.

Tackle obstacles as you did the big goals, breaking the bigger picture into smaller elements, bite-sized chunks which you can work with more easily.

For example, if you didn't get the new role or opportunity you were hoping for, resist despair, anger or self-recrimination. Instead, analyse what you could do differently next time to change the outcome. Break your action plan into pieces. Think about every part of the interview from how you presented yourself to the discussion. If you did your very best, you will of course feel disappointed, but you will need to move on from this feeling and turn it into a positive action, the next step on your journey.

If there are things that you know you could have done better, make yourself a plan to improve them. Perhaps get someone to help you. Do you need help or advice to overcome the obstacles you have identified above? A knowledgeable friend, an expert, accountant, marketeer or financier? Ask yourself if signing up for a course might help, or take a look at the myriad of free seminars on the web.

If there was a silver lining to this disappointment, what would it be? This can be a hard question especially if the let-down or obstacle was particularly hurtful or heart-wrenching. Nonetheless it is a question well worth putting to yourself, even if you don't come up with an answer immediately.

This well-worn but nevertheless insightful quote tells it like it is:

"Humans are like teabags, you never know how strong they are until you drop them in hot water" – Unknown

Often when faced with a difficult situation, it is very easy to obsess about why we can't possibly succeed with whatever we want to do. However, focusing on what we *can* do may well reveal a chink of light that offers a potential way out.

What can you do in the situation you are in? Put the situation in as positive a perspective as possible, one that will help you make plans.

It might help you to find a reassuring physical place to go to, or even a space in your imagination.

A talented sportsman I know has challenging difficulties to deal with at home, so when things are hard, he takes himself to a place of calm, albeit in his head. When he begins to feel distressed he sticks his headphones on for a few minutes, listens to something he loves and then, forgive the pun, he is ready to face the music. Tuning out the pain, and replacing it with something soothing is his way of getting back to homeostasis (that energetic, yet calm and ready for action, brain).

As we have discussed, when we are stressed and anxious, the transformative and innovative ideas are likely to elude us. However if we can find that calm yet energetic, homeostatic place in our brain, we are far more likely to be able to think our way out of difficulty or distress.

There are, of course, times when our brain needs to be able to make an instant adrenaline fuelled decision; when we're in physical danger for example. But as we've highlighted, when dealing with life's obstacles that aren't life-threatening, our thought processes are much more effective when they come from that alert but calm place.

One of my clients is particularly good at this. As a board-level executive for one of the largest companies in the world, she is masterful in getting to a place of homeostasis when the going gets tough. She has developed the discipline of not letting emotion cloud her judgment; instead she arms herself with the facts of any given scenario she is expected to deal with, delivering her views and stance with clarity and impact, inspiring her colleagues along the way. This ability to be cool, calm and collected in times of stress is not a talent she was born with, it is a skill she has worked hard to develop, one that has been invaluable to her.

ART OF POSSIBLE EXPANSION EXERCISE

What can you do?

Get active, write a plan, either a calming down plan or a plan in general; don't worry if your plan says "I need a plan", that's okay for now.

Write down what you think will help you get to a calmer place? How will you do it? What is your next step in developing your resilience (and brain plasticity)? Who or what calms you down?

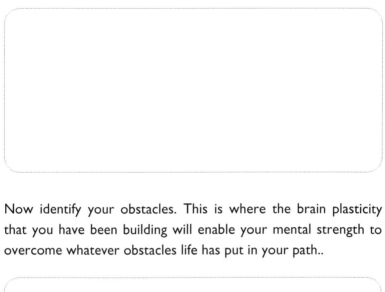

Now identify your obstacles. This is where the brain plasticity that you have been building will enable your mental strength to overcome whatever obstacles life has put in your path..

*

*

*

*

*

*

*

Be objective. How would a friend or someone who inspires you navigate these obstacles?

What do you think they might do first?

What will help you stand taller – both internally and externally?

Having noted your answers to the above questions, now think about how you are going to action some of these strategies and plans.

Take your brain to where your innovative thinking can occur, that place of calm yet energetic, your homeostasis.

When considering your plan of action it is important to try to keep the focus on the things that you can do, rather than those you think you can't. Think positively; make statements like "I can get out of this situation", "I can consult my colleague or mentor about this", "I can redo or adjust the project", "I can make this better, I can learn something".

This proactive approach will get the neurons bouncing in your brain, developing and strengthening its plasticity, creating new cells and getting you well on the way to realising your potential. Your brain will now be fully working with you to turn your plans into your goals.

Additional help:

Who is always guaranteed to make you smile or feel good regardless of whatever has happened to you?

Can you call them, text them or just think about a good time you spent with them? Contacting someone who inspires and supports you, even if you just talk to them in your mind, will help you get nearer to the energetic calm needed to be alert to new ideas.

As you will have learned by now, the brain will work most effectively for you when you ask it questions that are about the here and now, both in time and place.

Pose questions that are relevant to what is happening in the moment, be they about an obstacle you are overcoming or a strategy you are forming.

If you're planning a small fundraising event, for example, or want to run a global empire, every question and action has to be in the present. For it is through addressing the here and now that we can best harness the power of our brains and build plasticity, creating those invaluable new 'thinking' brain cells.

When I found myself up a mountain on my motorbike, in front of a very slippery patch of shale and a mighty steep bit of rock to ride up, my first thought was "I can't" – probably accompanied by a loud wail. However, once I had made myself calm down enough to reach a state of homeostasis (I didn't know it was that at the time), I was able to ask myself, "How am I going to find a way to do this? I've been trained by some of the best off-road bikers in the country, what would they do? I know that I am able to do this!" The bike was in a good position and still running, which made it easier, and I was just clear of a very wet and slippery looking bit.

I worked out what I could do, which was keep the bike in a low gear with consistent throttle all the way to the top, slipping the clutch when absolutely necessary, and having figured this out, I went ahead and got myself and the bike up the slope. I still found getting up that treacherous incline one of the hardest things that I have ever done, but the fact is I managed to do it. More importantly, I strengthened that crucial skill of getting comfortable (enough) with discomfort. I have since used this discipline in all sorts of situations.

Another practice that works when we've hit a metaphorical wall or difficulty is this:

It sometimes helps to think about what you have achieved so far, things that you have been proud of having done. This will refresh and remind you of your talents and skills, help you stand up taller, and become alert and energetic, ready to work on developing your brain's plasticity and moving towards living your own Art of Possible.

What have you achieved?

*

*

*

*

*

*

You could even just think of a good day (not a madly life-enhancing one, just one that you found satisfying), to buoy yourself up.

When there are events or things that are unwelcome or uncomfortable to you, it helps to remember that everything you experience, however difficult or distressing, has the potential to offer you growth, or learning, or both.

You are learning to become more comfortable with discomfort.

"Every single thing that has ever happened in your life is preparing you for a moment that is yet to come" – Anon

LIVING THE ART OF POSSIBLE

Amelia Jones is an inspirational and uplifting young lady who I am proud to know.

Amelia's little brother died from meningitis when he was just four years old. Amelia's mother has mental health issues and therefore Amelia often ran the household from a young age; cooking, cleaning and caring for her little brother. The little things that she did every day which most of us take for granted made a huge difference to both hers and her little brother's lives. Her childhood and education were blighted by the drugs and gun crime which dominated life in her neighbourhood. Amelia's spirit could so easily have been broken by the huge pain and suffering she'd experienced in her young life, but instead she chose not only to survive but to put her energy into making the most of her potential. She now has an apprenticeship with a large corporation and is studying for a degree.

"I have an opportunity that my little brother will never have. Always try to find the positives in a situation and ask, is it ever that bad?" – Amelia Jones

Amelia is extraordinarily resilient, she does a little something every day that takes her towards learning something new and developing herself, and she does each task with palpable joie de vivre and passion.

Riding on through the hard difficult days is tough. It takes discipline, self-control, mental strength and maybe even physical effort to work through the discomfort with resilience and stamina. And yet this ability to master resilience and stamina is a skill available to all of us and one of the lynchpins to living your Art of Possible.

LIVE THE ART OF POSSIBLE 'RESILIENCE WHEN THE GOING IS HARD' RECAP

YOU HAVE LEARNT:

- What are the hard challenges that you face now and may face in the future.

- What your next step is.

- Who can help you.

- What silver lining there might be to any obstacle.

- What you CAN do.

- How you can get to your calm and alert place when you are in turmoil.

- How to recall other challenges and difficulties that you have overcome.

- The importance of standing tall.

CHAPTER 13

USE YOUR FEAR

"You will face your greatest opposition when you are closest to your biggest miracle" – Shannon L Alder

There is a current theory that we are all driven by fear, either a fear of success or a fear of failure. I'm not certain that it's quite as clear cut as that, however I do know that fear plays a key role in the way we think about people, things and challenges. Our thinking really can impact upon the way we act, and it can stop us from doing things, in other words hold us back. On the other hand we can choose to acknowledge our fear and then carry on doing whatever it was that made us scared. If we can find a way to accept our fears and take them with us, regarding them as a minor hindrance (rather like having a mild cold) which just makes going about our daily business a little bit harder, our fears will not be able to stop us in our tracks.

Sometimes fear can feel utterly paralysing, so much so that we feel we can have no control over the situation. Yet it is almost always the case that we have the opportunity to control just a little bit of the predicament we find ourselves in, however small. And at the very least we can choose to take control over whether we are overcome by fear or not. Conquering our fears may seem easier said than done, but living *The Art of Possible* means that we recognise that we can take control over our lives.

Sometimes, we might use procrastination to mask the fear. But once we acknowledge that procrastination is merely the result of our brains requiring new information in order to proceed, we are in an ideal position to master our fears. Encouraging our brains to think in a calm cognitive way, rather than in emergency 'fight or flight' mode, reduces the power of fear to control our decisions.

There is no need for us to be fearful of fear itself, for it is a very natural, and often necessary response; a reaction that is designed to help us to survive. Fear is simply the result of our brains processing their very natural 'safe/not safe' assessment and reaching a 'not safe' conclusion. A warning to us to proceed with caution, or maybe that we need remove ourselves from the scenario PDQ. In the journey to living *The Art of Possible*, as in life generally, it is most likely our experience of the new and unfamiliar that will give rise to fear. Whether we are crossing a busy road, launching a new strategy, boarding a train late at night, in a café when someone we perceive to be a bit 'dangerous' walks in, or starting a company, fear is a natural response because it warns you that your brain is right at the boundaries of what you think you're capable of.

"People get frightened; better to have a go and it fail, than not try at all. If you want to have a go at something, have a go, but give it your best" — Paul Hammersley, regular Team GB European and UK Champion Gold Medal winner in water-skiing; slalom, jumps & trick

Understanding what triggers your fears and how you react to them helps you stay more focused on your end goal when you do become fearful. Knowing and accepting what makes you frightened, and how you are likely to respond to being scared, means that you can incorporate these fears in your journey. Yes, our fears may seem at times like unwelcome, uncomfortable and uninvited guests, but how much better to see them in this familiar way than being so frightened of them that we run away from our goals.

ART OF POSSIBLE EXPANSION EXERCISE

Consider:

If you can clearly identify your own response to fear, you'll have a greater ability to deal with these reactions when they occur. Being aware of the early signals of our brains going into fight or flight mode signifies that it's time to take action. Like a red warning light on a dashboard, the symptoms of the fear we experience at feeling uncomfortable are alerting us to seek more information, or do some more research, in order that we can make informed choices as to what to do next. What does fear do to you?

What happens to you when you're fearful?

Some suddenly feel cold, some laugh (yes, really), some freeze, some feel a strange, prickling sensation at the top of their backs, a bit like the hackles rising on a dog.

Do you find yourself unable to stop talking or gibbering?

Or do you internalise your fear and experience something physical such as nausea or butterflies in your tummy?

How does fear make you behave? How does it make you feel?

Arming ourselves with this knowledge about our fears, and the way we are likely to react to them, won't make the fear disappear. However we will have greater self-knowledge at our fingertips and will be able to ask our brains a helpful "What am I fearful about right now and what can I do about it immediately?" question.

We may find that right now we are unable to think about what we can do to help ourselves. Yet just this act of acknowledging and observing our vulnerable position will begin to unblock us, enabling us to look for new information that might assist us. Such calm thinking always produces an enhanced clarity of thought, an ideal state of mind in a crisis or tricky situation.

LIVING THE ART OF POSSIBLE

Take your time to deepen your thinking – what are you really afraid of?

Often our fear is not of the actual task ahead of us; whether it's giving a presentation, standing our ground about something, flying, falling in love or doing something for the first time. Instead we are more likely to be afraid

of the consequences of what we are about to do, e.g., we might get hurt physically or mentally, not be thought well of or perform badly.

Ask yourself again – what is it that makes you fearful?

If you find that you are more scared of the consequence of something happening, rather than the thing itself, think deeply about why this outcome concerns you so much.

What strategies could you deploy to at least mitigate the effects of this outcome?

Breaking the nature of your fears down into component parts can help you to understand them and then to face them down.

For example, when giving a presentation your fear can be more about the audience's reaction rather than the actual delivery of the presentation. In this scenario, you can't control how the audience will react to your presentation. However, you do have absolute control over your delivery, the information you deliver, how you deliver it, the way you look, whether or not you smiled, and how much preparation went into your presentation. The more you have considered all the elements that go into a successful presentation, the more control you will have gained over it, which in turn will lend greater composure and will have upped your chances of success.

When I was in training for the motorcycling trip in the Pyrenees I was fearful on a ridiculously regular basis. Not surprisingly, the fear wasn't about the riding of the bike or the motorbike itself, instead it was about falling off the bike and hurting myself. Sure, there were lots of reasons why I might fall off, but there were also many more reasons why I wouldn't – mostly things which were under my control. There were safety checks that I got into the habit of doing on the bike: brakes, gears and forks. I also developed something of a ritual around putting on protective clothing, which I saw as 'my armour'. And I never went out without a neck scarf, the obligatory lucky charm. I was still nervous, but my fear was not the type of terror which can render us unable to do what we are actually capable of. I did fall off many times; in fact so many I lost count, but my preparations, clear thinking and a bit of luck meant that I remained mostly unscathed with just a few bruises and sometimes hurt pride.

Ask yourself again, "What am I fearful about?"

Break it down. What are the component parts?

How can you regain some control of both the fear and the situation?

*

*

*

*

*

Remember once you have faced, acknowledged and taken steps to diminish the fear a little, you'll be in a much stronger place to 'face it down'. And once you have shown it who's the boss there's very little standing in your way!

LIVE THE ART OF POSSIBLE 'USE YOUR FEAR' RECAP

- That you need to take your fear with you as a necessary, if less welcome traveller, on your journey.

- What you are fearful about.

- How to identify your own response to fear.

- What fear does to you.

- That you can now take steps to regain control of the situation.

- And that you are ready to face down your fears and go for what you want.

CHAPTER 14

CONFIDENCE CAN BE BUILT

"I'm confident. I am. No I'm not. Yes, I am. Well, I am a bit." said a friend's child about a forthcoming sporting event.

It's what we grown-ups think sometimes too, and yet we rarely voice it.

Very early in my career, when I was facing the biggest career challenge in my work life to date, a well-intentioned person told me to "just be confident and be yourself". It was my first interview for one of the coveted places on the Marks and Spencer Management Training Programme. They might as well have told me to be an 'aardvark'; the fact was that I simply didn't know 'how' to be confident.

Confidence can be quite hard to define. For some it means being in control, for others it means feeling knowledgeable, and for many it just means having some kind of power. Confidence can certainly be elusive if we try to 'summon' it up on demand, as if trying to rub a lamp to call a genie. Yet more often than not, feeling confident simply means just feeling okay, rather than uncertain, with a given situation.

So, let's look at the things that make us feel more sure about whatever it is we are embarking upon.

WE CAN BE:

Prepared

Rehearsed

Calm (enough)

Well-presented

Informed

Wearing the right clothes or gear

Friendly

Approachable

Smiley

Standing tall

ART OF POSSIBLE EXPANSION EXERCISE

Make a list of the things that tend to help you feel a little stronger, a little bit more comfortable. These supportive props or things pave the way to beginning to feel confident when having a tremulous moment.

A colleague of mine was a dancer with the Royal Ballet. She recalled how her nerves often threatened to completely undermine her ability, and therefore her performance. Very often, this lack of confidence struck moments before she was about to go on stage.

Her solution was to use her anxiety instead of trying to ignore it. She would think about the butterflies in her stomach as flying in formation, as if she were directing them. This made her feel more in control, which in turn made her feel readier to face the challenge ahead and go on stage, where generally her confidence quickly returned.

Very often on your journey to living *The Art of Possible*, you will feel that fear is just part of the excitement of facing a new situation.

You can feel both fear and remain confident and prepared. And even if we do feel underconfident, we can use this emotion to help us to push just a little bit more towards regaining control.

Taking steps to be more prepared, rehearsed and looking the part means that we are ready to harness the adrenaline which may well be coursing through our veins.

You can take steps to 'feel' more confident with a little input and discipline. We can achieve extraordinary things even if we are underconfident, so long as we have developed the habit to not let our wavering confidence undermine us.

Use these questions to help you recognise what's going on in your mind and to get you into a more confident place.

Why might you not be feeling confident? For example, have you overlooked a necessary step in the journey towards your achievement? What can you do about it?

Acknowledge it.

Think about when you do feel confident. What confidence inspiring scenario is most vivid for you? It may be a work situation, something at home, being with friends or doing an activity.

Recall how you felt, as vividly as you can.

When do you feel at ease?

When do you feel in control?

If you can access how it feels to be confident, strengthening the neural pathways as you do so, it will be easier for you to rise above the anxiety you may have about your own abilities.

I work with a very successful CEO of a global corporation who suffered a horrid tragedy as a child. And this can sometimes still cause him moments of great anxiety, which can threaten to stop him in his tracks.

He has a rose garden that is his pride and joy. And when he feels his anxiety returning, prompted perhaps by having to make an opening plenary at a conference of thousands (he doesn't like crowds), he imagines being in his rose garden. The pleasure he associates with his garden releases the serotonin, dopamine and endorphins in his brain which in turn send feel-good signals to other cells. At this point all his preparation and rehearsal kicks in, and nobody knows that this successful man has to use this anchoring technique to get to an assured, confident place.

He admits that the anxiety doesn't completely dissipate, but just the act of thinking about somewhere where he feels at ease helps him regain control of the situation.

Being able to drop the angst down a notch or two gives us more clarity, enabling us to move ahead and do the job at hand more easily and convincingly.

FINDING YOUR OWN PLACE OF CONFIDENCE AND CALM:

In this scenario, practice makes perfect. Try it and see if it works for you.

Think about a place where you feel comfortable, at ease and confident. It might be with friends, chairing a meeting, walking the dog, making supper or being at a show.

Consider each of the senses:

What do you feel?

What or who can you see?

What or who can you hear?

Can you taste anything?

Can you smell anything?

Make this 'vision' as vibrant and vivid as you possibly can.

*

*

*

*

*

*

Practice thinking about being in this place and bring it to mind the next time you're feeling unconfident or anxious.

Confidence can sometimes feel as though it is a little elusive; however if we take steps to be prepared and act as if we were confident, we will begin releasing the punishing grip that underconfidence has on us.

Feeling underconfident can be extremely uncomfortable. But when we have taken steps to feel better about a challenging situation, we will feel more assured and able to do the tasks that lie before us. In other words we will feel more comfortable with discomfort. More at home with *The Art of Possible*.

Note:
Confidence is different for everyone and underconfidence can be extremely uncomfortable.

Not only do we have our own ways of reaching it, but we also have different ways of manifesting it. As we have seen, successful people who we may consider to be super confident may not be naturally so, indeed it is more than likely that they have worked very hard on cultivating this image of self-assuredness.

With discipline and effort we can all find our way to confidence.

LIVE THE ART OF POSSIBLE 'CONFIDENCE CAN BE BUILT' RECAP

YOU HAVE LEARNT:

- What makes your confidence waver.

- What are the particular situations where your confidence is most likely to fail you.

- What steps you can take to feel more prepared or be more able to deal with a scenario.

- What makes you feel confident.

- What will help you be more in control.

- How important it is to practice feeling confident.

PART 4

THE NEW WORLD – LIVING YOUR ART OF POSSIBLE

CHAPTER 15

BE HAPPY

This chapter is about generating happiness from small things in order to better enable you to do the big things. During my bike trip, in the midst of the mud, sweat and dirt of the trail, I spotted a hummingbird. I had never seen one up close in the wild and the grin in my helmet was huge. I got off my motorbike to take the time to get closer to this unfamiliar sight and was utterly mesmerised by the tiny, delicate and beautiful bird. It brought some well-needed perspective and inspiration.

I love the poem 'Leisure'...

What is this life if, full of care,
We have no time to stand and stare.

No time to stand beneath the boughs
And stare as long as sheep or cows.

No time to see, when woods we pass,
Where squirrels hide their nuts in grass.

No time to see, in broad daylight,
Streams full of stars, like skies at night.

No time to turn at Beauty's glance,
And watch her feet, how they can dance.

No time to wait till her mouth can
Enrich that smile her eyes began.

A poor life this if, full of care,
We have no time to stand and stare.

By W.H. Davies

This poem was written in 1911 and is still relevant over a hundred years later. Perhaps it is even more pertinent in today's world, one where technology has so revolutionised the way we live that we take even less time to stop and be present in the moment.

We regularly hear the people around us saying "I've no time"; time to be, to do or to think. If we are constantly occupied, constantly on the move, are we losing the chance to be happy in the moment? And crucially, are we allowing opportunities to pass us by, just because we are too busy to see them?

Finding time to stop and stare, to smell the coffee or the roses, or whatever the equivalent that works for you is, has always been important both to our well-being and our ability to think clearly and creatively. Taking time out to appreciate what a wonderful world we live in works the muscle of potential.

ART OF POSSIBLE EXPANSION EXERCISE

When can you schedule in a few moments in your day to just stop and be?

How can you stop, take time out of your day to enable you to just observe or watch, even for a few minutes each day?

"The true secret of happiness lies in taking a genuine interest in all the details of daily life" – William Morris

Remember that when we pause we are getting nearer to our energetic but calm place. And when observing the world around us more closely we are giving our brains new stimuli and resources to work with.

If you do just one thing today, find something that makes you happy and then just wallow in it, just for a few moments.

This might sound like stating the blooming obvious, but wallowing in life's pleasures, small and large, is one of the secrets to happiness. Being happy brings the additional gift of allowing you to be both calm and energetic, that magical place of homeostasis that makes it so much easier for you to realise your potential.

In the data-rich, fast paced environment in which we all live, our performance and productivity does benefit from the odd pause. The benefit of taking time out to just look and observe the world around us is that we are naturally taken back to that ideal state of homeostasis. Pausing in this way also gives us data and information which are likely to be new and different, even if all we are doing is just looking out of the window for a few minutes. Remember that each time you are observing others and seeking out the new, you will be strengthening your neural pathways, making the brain work harder and developing that muscle of discipline.

Sometimes when we seek success, happiness, fame, fortune (or for some even notoriety), what we are actually looking for is a route to inner peace.

I have consistently found that those who are able to live *The Art of Possible*, who are pursuing their goals and dreams and truly attaining what it is that they want, have developed an inner contentment that helped them reach their goals. Finding happiness on the inside will fuel what you are achieving on the outside. Of course it isn't always easy to find that sense of inner peace, particularly when life is throwing you difficult or distressing situations. Yet if you work to get your mind to that place that says 'I'm okay', you will find you have an invaluable tool for enabling you to realise your potential, so that you can do what you might once have believed was impossible.

List six little things that make you happy.

Nothing is too frivolous or too small to include in your list, provided it is something that makes you (rather than just those around you) genuinely happy.

It may be as simple as stopping for a cup of coffee or tea, taking a deep bath or a hot shower, looking at a beautiful view, watching wildlife doing its thing, having a creative meeting or remembering someone's smile.

1

2

3

4

5

6

"Your smile can change the world, but don't let the world change your smile" – Anon

Take time to include in your day one or two of the items on your list.

Happy is as happy does. Whilst neuroscience has yet to discover exactly what happens when we are happy, what it does know is that the level of neurotransmitters (chemical messengers) in the brain plays an important role in mood. Some experiments have linked higher levels of serotonin and dopamine in people who are happy, though there is not yet a general consensus on these findings. However, we all know that feeling happy affects both our own mood and influences other people's states of mind too.

When living your own Art of Possible, experiencing happiness can only be a good thing. Not only does happiness make us feel good, but it also gives our brain the space to innovate and create, as well as influencing others who might help us on our journey. For example when we smile, perhaps because we've just met a friend who we haven't seen in a long time, or something in our daily 'goings on' makes us smile, our neural pathways are strengthened.

The more we think about the situation the more of these pathways are created, further developing our neuroplasticity. In turn a positive feedback loop is reinforced in the brain and we feel happy. Or to put it another way, smiling stimulates our brain's mechanisms which in turn makes our brain feels good, causing it to send back messages to us to smile some more, which sends more 'happy' messages to the brain etc.

When we feel happy the strengthened neural pathways, neuroplasticity and creation of new brain cells develop a strong collaboration, allowing us to become far more able to be comfortable with discomfort. This fact in itself makes it worthwhile to try to welcome happiness into your life, or even just to think about smiling as often as possible.

Interestingly, kids smile on average about 400 times a day and a happy 'grown up' about 40 to 50 times a day, whereas the average person smiles just 20 times per day. This means that quite a lot of us aren't smiling nearly enough, a sad fact particularly when smiling has such a positive, nurturing effect on our brains. Smiling doesn't have to involve grinning so inanely that people start to cross the road when you walk by, it just means smiling naturally, allowing yourself to acknowledge the feeling of pleasure. Even if you're not grinning outwardly, you can 'smile' internally and feel happy. Developing the habit of smiling inwardly will be just as powerful as the physical smile, because it triggers the same effect in the brain.

Given that some people are naturally more smiley than others, it might take some work for some of us to remember to smile internally and externally. Like everything in this book, smiling is a discipline to hone, a skill to develop, and a very pleasurable one at that!

During the time I was writing this chapter, I was lunching with some colleagues when I happened to share the statistics about how often kids smile. We all agreed that the difference between the frequency of children and adults' smiling was fascinating. Except for one colleague, who had completely misheard the discussion. Perplexed, she said, in utter seriousness "But I didn't know that pigs could smile!"

The unintended consequence of the conversation was that it caused us a whole lot of unexpected mirth, we all fell about laughing and were all the happier for it! Silliness and a bit of laughter are always good for us.

Now, write down six big things that make you happy or are just plain fun.

It may be playing your favourite sport, having a drink or dinner with a good friend, going out to a show or a concert, finding a new client or a new deal, making a new friend or reading a book.

1

2

3

4

5

6

We can easily forget to make time for things that make us feel good, so make sure to build them into your calendar. Having something to look forward to will improve your mood and your optimism, and will make it so much easier for you to stay in that place of homeostasis, calm but energetic.

As Abraham Lincoln said:

"Most folks are as happy as they make up their minds to be"

I think he's right. And my favourite quote of all:

"A smile confuses an approaching frown" – Anon

– Hurrah to that!

LIVE THE ART OF POSSIBLE
'BE HAPPY' RECAP

- What made you happy in the last week.

- How to spend a few moments each day just reflecting, watching or noticing the world around you.

- What little things make you happy.

- What big things make you happy.

- When you can do these things that make you happy.

- That you need to remind yourself to smile, as often as possible – both inwardly and outwardly!

CHAPTER 16

BE TRULY ALIVE

When living *The Art of Possible*, we are working towards our own vision of success and living. This will naturally involve experiencing new and different things, which we will have to learn to get more comfortable with. For the fact is that encountering, and processing, the 'new' will make us feel new and different in ourselves, an experience which, if we welcome it into our lives, will bring about positive changes: to our brain power, our way of thinking and our life itself.

We are all alive, but feeling *truly* alive is what we should really be aiming for. The willingness to experience those moments which have the power to take our breath away, because they're so new to us and so different. That moment when we allow our brain to get to work on processing this 'new' experience or knowledge, and we begin to get comfortable with discomfort.

There is something extraordinary about feeling truly alive; it is exhilarating, we feel good, everything feels alright with the world, it's a magnificent place to be. We might also feel light-headed from the sheer adrenaline, feeling the blood coursing through our veins, the hair standing up on the back of our necks. We might even feel slightly nauseous due to the excitement..

"Life is not about the breaths we take but the moments that take it away" – Anon

When living *The Art of Possible* you will want to experience these moments of 'the new' as often as possible, challenging yourself right to the edge, and even beyond, what you think you are capable of.

ART OF POSSIBLE EXPANSION EXERCISE

Think back to the last time you felt alive; often this feeling occurs when we experience something new for the first time, or when we have a big success.

Conjure it up in your mind now;

Can you remember how it felt?

What did you do?

What did you see?

Who did you meet?

Once you set yourself off on the path of achieving your big goals, you will find yourself tackling many new things, and while that will be amazing, it will also feel a little 'hairy' or even scary, from time to time. So just hold on to your hat and dive into some new territory confident in the knowledge that your brain is cheering you along the way.

ART OF POSSIBLE EXPANSION EXERCISE

What can you do in the next month that you've never done before?

Doing something new not only makes us feel truly alive but it provides new stimuli for the brain, enabling it to come up with those fabulous transformative ideas and to develop its plasticity. So put yourself out there and welcome new opportunities and new people into your life. Live a bit dangerously!

Think back to the last occasion when you were spontaneous.

Think about how you can be spontaneous. Once you realise that you can discipline yourself to be spontaneous, new and perhaps unknown things will start to happen, and most important of all, you will have got yourself off the blocks.

Inevitably scheduling 'spontaneity' for Tuesday at 10am, will feel mighty peculiar at first. It may be that your first session involves nothing more than your feeling slightly silly or self-conscious, but at least you will be thinking about it. However, after a few weeks of having given yourself an hour to do something different or spontaneous, your thinking will have started to change. Because you have given it something new and different to think about, and the brain likes that! Consider:

When was the last time that you did something spontaneous?

How did it make you feel?

Was it something that you'd like to do again? If not, what would you do differently?

When was the last time that you did something that scared you?

Now think about how you felt after you had achieved it or even when you hadn't managed to.

Doing something spontaneous or something that scares you will continually build the muscle of being comfortable with discomfort.

"Get up and go for it, nothing comes from nothing"
– Jonathan Raggett, MD, Carnation Hotels

When I embarked on the challenging bike ride across the Pyrenees, I didn't finish the trip. I lasted a day and it was the hardest day of my life, both mentally and physically. I was initially disappointed, very angry and disheartened and felt that I'd failed. I stopped because it was evident that the trip was way above my level of capability and had I continued I would have been a danger to myself and others. In fact I had called the trip organiser three weeks previously to say I feared as much and to suggest that maybe a less technical or challenging ride might be more sensible – but he brushed my concerns aside! A good few weeks after my 'failure' I began to realise the pivotal effect the whole experience had on me; both personally and professionally. It suddenly dawned on me that rather than having been defeated I had succeeded, having done something way out of my comfort zone. Pushing myself beyond my fears, to the very limits of my endurance had taught me so many new things and I had met so many new and inspiring people along the way. That one day, that against all the odds I had managed to complete, turned out to be one of the greatest rides of my life!

Far from failing, I had succeeded in feeling truly alive (and had lived to tell the tale which afterwards I soberingly realised wasn't a given) and the effect was profoundly life-changing. It was a watershed moment, a sudden realisation that if you set your mind to something new with discipline and focus, the very thing that you previously considered utterly impossible is in fact possible, and within your reach.

When you get out of your comfort zone, it can at first feel mighty uncomfortable. But doing something very different and new will stretch you beyond what you thought was possible, into a new zone of possibility, encouraging your brain to seek out things that you perhaps didn't know you were suited to.

And then we innovate and create in ways that we haven't before.

ART OF POSSIBLE EXPANSION EXERCISE

Don't think too deeply about this exercise, it is designed to stir up your thinking patterns.

Think back to the last occasion when you surprised yourself.

Why did it surprise you?

Do you want to do it again?

What do your two answers above reveal to you?

When was the last time that you surprised others?

What things can you do today or tomorrow that you don't usually do?

Our brains are used to forming such very well-worn patterns that it's very good to shake them out of what they know, encouraging them to form new pathways, new habits and new routines.

Challenging our brains with the 'new' in this way will develop our thinking, create new neural pathways, stimulating our greatest ideas to rise to the surface.

Feeling alive, scaring yourself, being spontaneous and doing something new will continually develop your ability to be comfortable with discomfort, and get you back to that place of homeostasis ready for the next big thing!

LIVE THE ART OF POSSIBLE 'BE TRULY ALIVE' RECAP

- When you last felt truly alive.

- How it felt to be alive in this way.

- When the last time was that you did something that scared you.

- When you last did something spontaneous.

- The need to plan an activity or experience in the next month that will truly get you out of your comfort zone.

CHAPTER 17

KEEP THE MOMENTUM

"Life is like riding a bicycle. To keep your balance, you must keep moving" – Albert Einstein

Every day counts. Today is the first day of the rest of your life. How will you use it?

Are you truly present in the here and now? We all know people who seem to be so rooted in the past that it seems as if they are actually living there. This nostalgia will be noticeable from what they choose to talk about, the stories they want to tell of the life that they once had, rather than the life they currently have. As was once said:

"You can't start the next chapter in your life if you keep rereading your last one" – Anon

Once you have embarked upon your quest to achieve your goal, you will find that, rather like riding a bike, keeping the momentum going is crucial. This momentum will keep you progressing towards living your own Art of Possible, making the tough days less of a struggle and making the easy days even simpler. It is easier to stay in the here and now if we are doing what we are passionate about.

ART OF POSSIBLE EXPANSION EXERCISE

What are you passionate about right now?

Have you done something today that is related to what you feel passionate about?

When we put off or don't do what we are passionate about, we are missing an opportunity to realise our potential. Reaching your goal may involve taking smaller steps than we'd envisaged, may mean it takes longer for us to get there; however it will be a small price to pay if we are truly passionate about our quest.

The fact is that we rarely regret the things that we did do, it's usually what we didn't do that weighs on our minds. Therefore do what you can do today to take you closer towards your goals and passions.

"Passion, determination and optimism goes a long way"
– Stephen Fear, The Fear Group.

List six things that you would like to achieve this year:

1

2

3

4

5

6

List six things that you can do this week, things that will take you a step closer to your passions and desires and help you keep your momentum going:

1

2

3

4

5

6

"Grasp the nettle and get on with it. Be courageous and crack on" – Tracey Curtis-Taylor, Aviatrix

List six things that you will do this month that will take you closer to your passions and desires:

1

2

3

4

5

6

The answers that you have formulated above will provide food for thought for your strategic plan.

Your internal passions can impact hugely on the reality that you create externally. Your passions will often be the fuel that drives you to your goals and ambitions. The power of passion is immense. We only need to look at history books to see that revolutions were started, feuds ended, scientific and medical breakthroughs were enabled or significant changes were made to society more often than not because of someone daring to have a dream and a passion.

Harnessing your passion to create forward momentum will in turn create the frisson of energy that will make the journey towards the accomplishment of your goals easier.

The Pixar animated movie *Finding Nemo* is a lovely story about a fish father searching for and finding his lost son. The Dad is utterly driven throughout his search by his passion, and of course his love for his son. The motto of the movie is " Just keep swimming" , sung to the father by another fish, particularly when the going has gotten arduous. " Just keep swimming" means enabling yourself to continue striving and persevering with your goals and ambitions, even though you might be scared. This moving forward is of paramount importance when striving to live the life of *The Art of Possible*. In the movie, it didn't matter that the father was a little fish in a big sea, nor that his companion was a bit 'crackers'. What really counted was that the father had passion, tenacity and the ability to enlist support from others, including a group of fish who he encouraged to work with him to break the net in which they were all trapped.

Tenacity, persistence and passion will get you a very long way. All the successful people I've been fortunate enough to interview and work with display this "keep on swimming" quality, an ability to keep moving towards their goals during the good days, the bad days and the downright ugly days.

As a species, we have a natural ability towards survival and resilience, which means that perseverance and tenacity are well within our capability, provided we choose to use our skills, 'up our game' and keep moving forwards.

SMALL WINS: LIVING THE ART OF POSSIBLE

I met a real tough guy recently who said to me, somewhat surprisingly, "Never underestimate the power of making your bed". And then he went on to explain, "At the end of a rotten day, to come back to a well-made bed means that you did achieve something in the day". It won't surprise you to learn that he served in the armed forces.

Consider what daily action you might adopt as a means of moving towards living your Art of Possible – the six things you listed may give you some insights towards what this might be. Make sure that it's something that inspires you to do your best work and move forward towards your aspirations.

*

*

*

*

*

*

LIVE THE ART OF POSSIBLE 'KEEP THE MOMENTUM' RECAP

YOU HAVE DISCOVERED:

- What you are passionate about.

- Whether you've done something today that ignites your passion.

- What you can do daily to keep the momentum going, something simple.

- The importance of continuing to strive and persevere.

- Keeping up the momentum

CHAPTER 18

SHARE & MENTOR

"When you give away everything that you know, more will come back to you" – Paul Arden

When we start out on a new path other people will notice the change in us; whether it's a sparkle in your eye, a renewed vigour or maybe just something they can't put their finger on.

It is inspiring to observe another person striving to achieve something new or different, sometimes just witnessing someone else travelling down their own road to success is enough to spur others on to change or renew their own path.

When we are on a new personal journey, often the best way to really deepen our knowledge about what we are discovering is to teach someone else. Especially when we are learning something new. Try to teach someone else what you have learnt; if you succeed in teaching them then you will know that you are well on the way to mastering the subject yourself. If it's still a bit unclear you may need some more practice at it or to do a bit more research. If we share the very thing that we are trying to master ourselves, it sure alerts us as to whether we know what we are doing or not.

If you are successful in any area of your life, the chances are that someone, somewhere, helped, taught or just encouraged you along the way; whether a teacher, colleague, boss, friend or family member.

"To be an inspiring leader, you have to be inspired by others connecting, engaging and sharing, with honesty and warmth" – Sharon Hanooman, CEO, Women's Health & Family Services (Charity)

You may have learned new skills and knowledge from those that have helped you; they may even have given you great experiences.

Or they may have just believed in you, like no-one else ever had.

They may have given you some time and TLC. Generally the ones who have made a difference in our lives are the ones who cared.

"Mentoring is all about people – it's about caring, it's about relationships and sensitivity" – René Carayol MBE

ART OF POSSIBLE EXPANSION EXERCISE

Name six people who have taught you something worthwhile:

1

2

3

4

5

6

Name six people who inspired you and also those that made you feel special or able.

1

2

3

4

5

6

What did they do for you, that you could do in turn for someone else?

Who is that someone else?

Who can you mentor or spend time with? It may be on a one-to-one basis or in a group scenario, formal or informal.

Perhaps for a charity or community group?

When you give back, you will find that your own journey towards living *The Art of Possible* will be so much richer for it. And of course, with the muscle of potential developed still further.

LIVE THE ART OF POSSIBLE 'SHARE AND MENTOR' RECAP

YOU HAVE LEARNT:

- Who inspired you.

- How to share your skills and knowledge.

- Who you can in turn inspire.

- Who you can mentor.

- How and when you can mentor them.

GREATER HEIGHTS

WHAT'S NEXT FOR YOU?

"Never underestimate the power of being near to someone doing something amazing, it will make you expect more of yourself" – Matt Brittin, President EMEA Business and Operations, Google

You are that person doing something amazing. Having picked up this book and tasked yourself with the job of discovering what is possible for you, you will now be able to expect more of yourself as well as those around you.

When we realise and see glimpses of what is possible for us through discipline and application, we see that it is a very exciting place to be. It can be spine-tingling, mind-blowing, overwhelming and sometimes terrifying when we discover talents that we never knew we had. When we find ourselves achieving things that we considered to be way beyond our capability, we move from our comfort zone into a considerable amount of discomfort, only to discover that it's actually okay at the other side. After a while we will have to leave this comfort zone too of course, onto the next bit of discomfort and then into the next comfort zone etc. This, as you now know, is what living *The Art of Possible* means. Through harnessing the amazing computer that is your brain you will be developing your thinking power, creating new neurons, achieving homeostasis (calm but alert) in order to cope better with the stresses and difficulties that life throws at you - and your life will be richer for it.

By exposing yourself to as much new data and information as you can and as many new experiences and activities as you can, your brain will work harder both *with* you and *for* you. Living *The Art of Possible* is as joyful as it is hard, and as enhancing as it is challenging.

The eighteen step process combined with the Living *The Art of Possible* recaps enabled you to realise your Art of Possible – harnessing the latest in neuroscience to make the impossible, possible.

YOU HAVE DEVELOPED & LEARNED:

- How to grow your brain.

- What success is for you.

- What you want.

- That procrastination is okay.

- New experiences + new thinking = new results.

- That random thoughts can provide concrete answers.

- When you acknowledge your strengths you can grow them.

- That curiosity pays off and to capitalise on learning.

- How to shake off doubts.

- How to use your talents to get unstuck.

- The power of happiness.

- That attention to detail pays off.

- How to feel truly alive.

- To practice resilience when the going is hard.

- How to use your fear.

- That confidence can be built.

- How to keep the momentum.

- The importance of sharing & mentoring.

You have taken yourself right to the edges of what you may have considered to be your limitations, and pushed through them to spur you on to greater heights.

By defining your success and realising the potential that lies within you, you will have found that what you previously thought impossible will become possible.

What is next?

I salute you and wish you an incredible journey.

ACKNOWLEDGEMENTS

It would have been impossible for me to write this book without help from many, many people.

The book is filled with insights and observations from stories and experiences that have been kindly shared with me over the years.

Some people are named in the book, some people disguised.

To the clients, friends, family and strangers that I've met; I am truly grateful, it is you who inspired me.

Jacq Burns for her encouragement and support and literally and metaphorically holding my hand all the way from start to finish.

Jamie Crocker for wonderfully capturing the illustrations that I had in my head.

Katie Sampson for magical editorial input and boundless moral support.

Megan Sheer for making the book look just the way I wanted it to.

To those who believed in me, especially when I didn't, in particular my gorgeous sister Elly Hanna, Rachel Pedrithes and my late grandfather Ian Poulson.

So many provided comment, insight, endless inspiration and encouragement: James Orrell, Kathy Harper, Paul Hammersley, Rob Jonas, Ashok Vaswani, Rick Parry, Karen Atkinson MBE, Robb Gravett, Billy Ward, Clive Kornitzer, Jo James, Anthony Thomson, Jonathan Raggett, Rebecca Souster, Stephen Fear, Tracey Curtis-Taylor, Sir John Whitmore, Dr Rachael Ancliff, Dr Phil Ancliff, John Kaufman, Ray Chandler, Deanna Chandler, Hoda M Ali, Sharon Hanooman, John Stoneman, Natalie Ojaveh, Sally Saunders-Makings, Ollie Makings, Grant Allaway, Karen Taylor, Darren Levy, Tessa Oversby, Olivia Haslehurst, Maria Gillies, Karoline Molberg, Donna Gray, Martin Wittering, Rachael Bartels, René Carayol MBE and Tricia Pritchard.

To my husband Robin and my daughters, Tabi and Sophia who have had to live with this book almost daily for the last year or so. This book is better for your challenging yet gentle encouragement and your acute insights. Thank you for your love and support.

Thank you all.

ABOUT THE AUTHOR

Kate Tojeiro is an executive coach and facilitator to the boards, senior executives and teams at some of the largest global organizations, and also some of the most cutting-edge, organically grown start-ups. She has built up a string of prestigious FTSE 100 and Fortune 500 clients and is a visiting faculty member at The Judge Business School. She has formed a reputation for developing some of the world's most successful and illustrious leaders and the next generation of rising stars.

She is the Managing Director of progressive leadership consultancy X fusion, a regular fixture on BBC radio and a voice in the media.

Kate lives in Cambridgeshire with her family, a collection of animals large and small, and a motorbike.

CONTACT US

If you would like to tell us about how you are living *The Art of Possible*, share your experiences or contact us, we would love to hear from you;

www.theartofpossible.co.uk

e. art@theartofpossible.co.uk

twitter. @katetoj

instagram. katetoj

#theartofpossible

You can also find Kate Tojeiro at X fusion

www.the-x-fusion.co.uk

e. info@the-x-fusion.co.uk

NOTES

10% of all book proceeds will be donated to NACOA.

The National Association for Children of Alcoholics (NACOA) is a registered charity (No. 1009143), founded in 1990 to address the needs of children growing up in families where one or both parents suffer from alcoholism or a similar addictive problem. This includes children of all ages, many of whose problems only become apparent in adulthood.

NACOA has four broad aims:

1. To offer information, advice and support to children of alcohol-dependent parents

2. To reach professionals who work with these children

3. To raise their profile in the public consciousness

4. To promote research into:
    *   the particular problems faced by those who grow up with parental alcoholism
    *   the prevention of alcoholism developing in this vulnerable group of children

1 in 5 children in the UK are affected by their parents' drinking

Alcohol problems often become the family secret, hidden from the outside world. This leaves children isolated and alone with no one to turn to.

NACOA is here to help and together we can give them the chance of a brighter future.

You can find out more about the wonderful work that NACOA does at www.nacoa.org.uk